LENDING AND SECURITIES

A practical guide to the principles of good lending

Christopher Parry

institute of financial services

UMIST

CIB Publishing
c/o The Chartered Institute of Bankers
Emmanuel House
4-9 Burgate Lane
Canterbury
Kent
CT1 2XJ
United Kingdom

Telephone: 01227 762600

CIB Publishing publications are published by The Chartered Institute of Bankers, a non-profit making registered educational charity.

The Chartered Institute of Bankers believes that the sources of information upon which the book is based are reliable and has made every effort to ensure the complete accuracy of the text. However, neither CIB, the author nor any contributor can accept any legal responsibility whatsoever for consequences that may arise from errors or omissions or any opinion or advice given.

Trademarks

Many words in this publication in which the author and publisher believe trademarks or other proprietary rights may exist have been designated as such by use of Initial Capital Letters. However, in so designating or failing to designate such words, neither the author nor the publisher intends to express any judgment on the validity or legal status of any proprietary right that may be claimed in the words.

Typeset by Kevin O'Connor

Printed by Bookcraft (Bath) Ltd., Midsomer Norton, Somerset.

© Chartered Institute of Bankers 1999

ISBN 0-85297-510-4

Lending and Securities

This textbook has been written for both students and practitioners of the subject. It has been written to a syllabus drawn up by subject experts, including current senior practitioners, which forms part of the Diploma in Financial Services Management (DFSM). This qualification is administered by the Institute of Financial Services, a wholly owned subsidiary of The Chartered Institute of Bankers and is awarded jointly by The CIB and the University of Manchester Institute of Science and Technology (UMIST). The role of UMIST in this partnership is to benchmark all aspects of the delivery of the DFSM, including this text, to first year undergraduate standard.

Though written to a syllabus specific to the DFSM it is intended that this text will serve a useful purpose for anybody studying for a business or finance-related qualification. Furthermore, this book will serve as an excellent reference tool for practitioners already working in this or related fields. All books in the DFSM series reflect the very latest regulations, legislation and reporting requirements.

Students of the DFSM will also receive a separate Study Guide to be used in conjunction with this text. This Study Guide refers the reader to further reading on the topic and helps to enhance learning through exercises based upon the contents of this book.

This book is dedicated to the following people who have been and continue to be the rocks in my life.

Mum and Dad   Don't take the bits about repayment too seriously! Thanks for the gardening and everything else.

Jenna and Matthew   Neither are good credit risks but their account with the Bank of Dad is always in credit.

Lisa   My wife whose support for this project was unstinting. Let me explain again what I mean by a "loan".

Bethan   The newest and littlest Parry. You beat the book by two weeks and I hope you like it. Speak to your sister about getting money out of Dad – she's the expert!

CONTENTS

	Introduction	1
1	**The Canons of Lending**	**10**
	1 The lending equation	12
	2 Practical applications	22
2	**Customers**	**39**
3	**Lending Facilities**	**59**
	1 Liquidity needs	60
	2 Revolving credit	61
	3 Loan accounts	72
	4 Business borrowing	83
4	**Financial Statements**	**95**
	1 Assets	97
	2 Liabilities	102
	3 Management accounts	115
5	**Ratio Analysis**	**121**
	1 Alfa Ltd – Standard Accounting Pro-formas	121
	2 Capital structure	126
	3 Asset utilization	128
	4 Profitability	129
	5 Liquidity	131
	6 Investment	132
6	**General Principles of Security**	**142**
	1 Security values	143
	2 Forms of security	145

7   **Land**   **155**

    1   Land ownership   157

    2   Procedure for taking security   161

8   **Other Forms of Security**   **166**

    1   Fixed and floating charges   166

    2   Life policies   169

    3   Stocks and shares   176

    4   Guarantees and indemnities   178

    5   Goods and produce   180

    6   Conclusion   181

Appendix 1: The Trick is Knowing When Not to Lend   **183**

Index   **185**

INTRODUCTION

Where shall we start? A useful place to begin any new area of study is to check that we know what we are studying and what we want to achieve. The dictionary definition of *lending* is:

1. *To grant the use of a thing on the understanding that it, or its equivalent, shall be returned;.*

   or

2. *To allow the use of money at interest.*

And, similarly, *security* is defined thus:

1. *Thing deposited as a guarantee of undertaking or loan, to be forfeited in the case of default.*

   or

2. *Document as evidence of a loan.*

For an interesting view on security perhaps you ought to have a quick look at Shakespeare's *A Merchant of Venice*. One of the central characters is a moneylender and he had an unusual concept of security.

O.K. – so we know what we are studying, but how about what we want to achieve? Aside from the stock student answer "passing the exam", the following is surely a good finishing point. The successful student will be able to:

- Adopt and apply the principles of good lending; this involves being comfortable with the concepts of safety (stability), liquidity (the ability to repay) and profitability (the continued ability to maintain repayments). Good lending also involves knowing when to take some form of security and when to realize it.

- Identify the lending services and analyse any special considerations appropriate to the various types of borrowers. It can be argued that all lending is the same. The successful student will be comfortable with the extent to which this is true and, equally importantly, when it is not.

- Demonstrate an ability to recognize the causes and warning signs for potential bad debts: the monitoring of facilities is as important as the original approval. Lending can go wrong very quickly – the best lenders spot the danger signs early.[1]

- Have an understanding of the stages and means of recovery action for bad and doubtful

[1] Which a number of lenders re-learnt in the early 1990s.

debts: those lenders who do not spot lending going wrong end up doing a lot of recovery.

● Interpret balance sheets and the use of supporting financial information as a tool of the lender: a business communicates its health, or otherwise, through its accounts. Every lender needs to be able to speak the language of the balance sheet even if only in the most rudimentary form.

● Understand the general principles of security sought by lenders: the availability of security is not a reason to lend. However, security does reduce the lender's risk. This can be an important factor in the decision-making process.

● Demonstrate an understanding of the procedures for the taking, discharge and realization of the types of security commonly offered.

The above looks and sounds like distinct elements. *They are not.* Lending is a tapestry. And like the finest tapestry one loose thread will cause the whole body to unwind. You cannot lend without having an awareness of all the aspects. Given that your main concern (at the moment) is passing an exam, please do not fall into the trap of trying to spot questions from previous exam papers and ignore chunks of the syllabus.

You cannot pass without knowing the entire syllabus.

Therefore it is fair to say that all the above are part of a process which, if you can master it, will stand you in good stead throughout your financial services career, and beyond.

That process is *risk management*[2].

Risk: *the chance or possibility of danger, loss, injury, etc.*

The level of risk is normally expressed by percentages and probabilities. The event with a probability of 1 is certain to happen. The event with a probability of 0 is impossible.

In his recent book Peter Bernstein[3] tells us that the word risk derives from the Latin word *riscare* meaning *to dare*. And all lending is a form of a dare. It is a gamble on the success of a borrower. In return for taking any risk the lender expects a return in the form of interest payments. There is an implicit relationship between the level of risk and the level of return which can be expressed as *"the higher the potential risk the greater the return required for taking that risk"*.

Management: *the process of controlling and/or manipulating a situation to achieve a desired goal.*

The process of management is most important for outcomes that are neither certain nor impossible.

The text that follows will endeavour to introduce you to *risk management* as it relates to lending in as practical a manner as possible, but please do not close your eyes to the underlying process.

---

[2] You *will not* be examined on the remaining pages of the introduction but they do give a basic theoretical framework.
[3] *Against the Gods* (Wiley 1997).

Risk management

Is a multi-phase process:

Identification

This involves considering the type of risk. There are several different types of risk including credit risk, economic risk, and political risk etc. The main concern to lenders is obviously credit risk:

The possibility that money lent will not be repaid.

However, every business is exposed to various levels of different types of risk and astute lenders consider all the risks a business is exposed to. For example, a business exporting to the USA but not considering foreign exchange cover would be taking needless exchange rate risk because it would probably be paid in dollars, the value of which fluctuates against sterling.

Assessment

All lenders assess every proposal to determine the overall risk to themselves. There are four levels of risk:

- Trivial;
- Minor;
- Major;
- Catastrophic.

Trivial is a level of loss that is not going to impinge adversely on profitability. Minor risks will affect a balance sheet in the year it occurs and major will affect the balance sheet for several years. Catastrophic risk could destroy a company. Obviously no lender should take on risks that would be catastrophic.

In addition to the levels of risk there is also the elements of every risk. These are *peril* and *hazard*.

Peril can be defined as the cause of loss and hazards are those factors that make loss more likely. These are physical, moral and morale.

For example for every lender there is the possibility that the business will fail. Every proposition should address those hazards that could make failure more likely:

Physical	Competitors, New products;
Moral	Dishonesty of borrower;
Morale	Commitment of borrower.

We will see in later chapters that all these matters are considered through such things as credit references, business plans, SWOT analyses and security.

Management

There are three main methods of managing risk.

The first is to not accept the risk – avoidance – thus no lending, no losses. But no risk, no return. A lender needs to know when to say no. There are some propositions that are too risky and no amount of potential return should make them attractive. Bankers should not be greedy and, although banks must lend to survive, not all lending is desirable.

The second method is risk transference. This is used often with very large loans where the loan is syndicated and several lenders each bear a proportion of the risk. For example the Channel Tunnel was not funded by one large bank but by over twenty.

Thirdly we have risk retention. Risk retention can best be explained by considering forms of insurance. The law says we need to have some forms of motor insurance. Insurance companies offer cover beyond this level. We can choose risk retention – stick with third party, fire and theft cover – or risk transfer – purchase fully comprehensive cover. If we do not purchase fully comprehensive we have retained the risk. This is what happens for the majority of bank lending. It is here that proactive management becomes vital.

*Articles appear in the press regularly – read them. Some will have little or no relevance to your current studies but some will enhance your understanding and thus improve your chances of passing the exam **and** learning something.*

Before moving forward it is perhaps important to spend a few minutes concentrating on an important cog in the lending process – you. It is you who will assess the proposal, and you who will make the decision. Yes and you who will "carry the can" if that decision proves incorrect. Fortunately, for you, your employer, their customers and their shareholders, you will not be let loose on customers with lending authority[4] until you have been properly trained in the lending process. This takes us to the heart of a much-discussed question – "Is lending a science or an art?[5]" and the quip "Good lenders are born not made". Is there more to the decision-making process than a series of techniques? If no, anybody can become a good lender – if yes, then some will be precluded from being good lenders. It has been suggested that some never make good lenders because of some lack or flaw in their pre-existing decision-making processes. Let us therefore consider the process through which we, as people, make decisions.

Firstly it is important to stress that you are already a decision maker. Have you ever asked yourself "Why did I do that?" I suspect that you do that only when you have made a mistake. As you reflect on that mistake, you will sometimes learn a lesson – other times you do not. Why? We will consider the answer in depth in Chapter 3.

Each one of us operates consciously and subconsciously – we decide to walk or run or talk but we do not decide to breathe or pump blood. In the same way, by the time we reach

---

[4] Remember the converse of authority is responsibility.
[5] Of which more later.

maturity we have developed a subconscious framework of mental processes which act as our decision-making process for much of what we do. These *heuristics* are essential because they allow us to take the inputs from a complex environment and simplify them into a useable format.

There are several problems with our heuristics:

1) We have only a limited capacity for storing information. (How much do you remember from your third year at senior school in terms of what you learned?) Unlike today's computers we cannot upgrade our hard drive when it becomes full, or store data on a detachable floppy disk.

2) We have only limited brainpower. To stretch our computing analogy further we start off with a 486 or a Pentium and that's it. We can maximise the way we use our brains through education but we cannot change from being moderately intelligent to genius through hard work. Why is this a problem? Well the problem is that we do not really believe that we are as limited as we are, and this tends to lead to overconfidence in ourselves and in our decisions.

This is disastrous for lenders! And it is essential that we, as conduits, strive to develop a structure to decision making that is consistent and logical while being flexible and adaptive. How can we do this? By understanding our current heuristics. And there are strong arguments for looking at the two main heuristics we consistently use. The first of these is the *representational heuristic*. Here we subconsciously look for similarities between situations and develop outcomes from the similarities. For example, if a couple has two children, both girls, and are expecting a third child there is a tendency to expect that this too will be a girl. This ignores the **fact** that gender is random and there are practically equal probabilities of a boy or girl.

The practical application for you is probably clear. As a lender we look for proposals that are similar to those we have approved before and that have been successful, i.e. if one of your customers is a successful greengrocer your representational heuristic puts a tick in a mental box that says greengrocers are a good risk. If you have six successful greengrocers you have six mental ticks. A proposal comes in from a potential customer who wants to set up as a greengrocer and your subconscious says "Greengrocers good". Overreliance on this could lead to lending without a proper, complete appraisal of the specific proposal.

An alternative scenario is the successful greengrocer (with a mental tick) applying for a facility to start a garage. Your heuristic can again push you down the road of "Fred is successful – Fred will always be successful".

The opposite is also true. If we have built up a mental box which says "Lending to people with green eyes is bad" [6] then we run the real risk of missing a good proposal because the potential borrower has green eyes.

The second main heuristic is the *availability heuristic*. We have, as has been said, limited capacity and we tend to make greatest use of the most available (most recent or most dramatic)

[6] With apologies to all green-eyed people. No inference of lack of credit worthiness is intended or implied.

information in our memories irrespective of whether or not it is the most relevant. There are several factors causing this. Perhaps the most important is: How did we receive the information?

Read it

Written information is good. By and large a great deal of care has gone into its preparation. Its accuracy, while not guaranteed, is often high. On the negative side some (many?) of the proposals made to us will have been meticulously prepared and presented to disguise a lack of content. There is a major danger here for lenders in that we get often get carried away with the packaging.

The main drawback with written information is that it can be bland. This blandness often encourages us to relegate the information to the back of our minds

> *What did last week's head office memo say about lending to businesses with an "I" in the title?*

where it becomes less and less available as time passes regardless of how important it is. One senior lender of my acquaintance used to keep an index of all head-office memos for future use because he knew how poor his long-term memory was.

Here is a further example of the availability heuristic by way of a question.

> *King Harold died in 1066 with an arrow through his eye. When and how did William the Conqueror die?[7]*

There is a strong possibility that you do not know. Harold's death was dramatic and that sticks in our mind and is readily available.

Told it

We are far more likely to remember something we have been told. This is enhanced by our concept of the person telling us. For example, the share tip of a well-trusted friend or a **"Cert!"** in the 3.30 at Doncaster may be acted on whereas the same information from a newspaper or a third party not known to you will be rejected. Another example relates back to our school days. Which subject did you like most and which did you hate? What memories do you have of the staff involved?

The danger with the information we are told is misunderstanding – "I know you understand what you think I said but I don't think you understand what I think I said."

Sadly we often remember incorrect information told to us by a respected colleague at the expense of the correct information in last month's instruction notices.

Interactive

The more of our senses we use to process information the more we remember.

[7] Answers on a postcard – I forget as well.

This is a decided advantage. The more *relevant* data we have the better will be the quality of our decision making and the more confident we can be in it. However there is the danger of information overload and the necessity to winnow the relevant from the padding. Most large Plcs use the interactive heuristic in their presentations to investment analysts. These presentations are designed to update the analysts on the company's current performance, its plans and expectations. This intimacy helps to reinforce positive feelings about the company and hopefully a "buy" recommendation. The cynics would say that the better the presentation, the worst the truth. This is obviously an example of a heuristic developed by somebody who has made a judgement (or a number of judgements) based on presentations that ultimately failed to match up to reality. The danger here of course is that the *feelings* engendered can cause us to overlook something that may otherwise have been a cause for concern.

In spite of the dangers, the interactive delivery channel is highly useful and as lenders we can make it work for us by visiting our customers (and potential customers) in-situ. I would go so far as to say that rule of thumb three[8] is:

> *Don't lend if you haven't visited.*

Obviously this is far more relevant (and far more practised) in business as opposed to personal lending.

An important factor, which affects how we utilize information, is our level of understanding of the data we have and this links into our limited capacity. If we are uncomfortable with ratio analysis we will often relegate the importance of the ratios because we do not really understand them. The opposite is, of course, true. Those who "are wizards with figures" tend to display overreliance on the figures (the quantitative data) to the detriment of the qualitative data. A good lender will balance the two.

Dealing with our heuristics

Given the above you are probably beginning to think:

> *OK, how do I dump my heuristics?*

Really you do not need to. You do, however, as lenders, have to be aware of them, and how you rely on them because they can lead to inconsistencies within your judgements. There are two types of judgmental inconsistencies. The first is *random inconsistencies*. These are the inconsistencies arising because of transitory conditions such as boredom or mood. Research suggests that if we are depressed we rely very heavily on our availability heuristic and will retrieve negative facts and apply them to situations. This means that we might be assessing a proposal (in a down frame of mind) and turn it down because we remember a similar deal that failed two years ago and not the half a dozen similar deals that succeeded.

More important, however, is *systematic inconsistencies* – these are judgement errors you continue to make.

Consider the following:

[8] Hopefully by now you are saying to yourself that these rules of thumb are an alternative form of representational heuristic. You are of course right.

You are offered two choices:

a) A certain £8,000 or a choice that offers an 85% chance of winning £10,000 and a 15% chance of winning nothing.

Most people are risk adverse and will take the guaranteed £8,000. Some are risk takers and would take the bet. What would you do?

In reality most people will take the bird in the hand and avoid the risk of gaining nothing. Some (those who are particularly risk taking) will go for the £10,000 but most will not. Are we mostly risk adverse then? If we are it is bad news for profits in coming years. Consider a second question from a lending point of view.

b) A business you are lending to is in difficulty. The situation at present is that you can call in the receivers and have a guaranteed loss of £8,000 or allow the business to trade for another month and have a 85% change of losing £10,000 and a 15 % chance of losing nothing.

One would think that, as most people go for the certain profit, most would go for the certain loss. Sadly no. Whereas most people do indeed go for the certain profit, most go for the chance of no loss. In "techo-speak" we are risk adverse in the face of gains and risk positive in the face of losses. This could be very bad news for lenders. And indeed one of the major causes of losses to lenders is the tendency to fail to get out at the right time. Many lenders have ended up with far more egg on their face than they needed to because they refused to believe that a project they had approved could/would fail.

It is important that we are aware of our heuristics and how they affect us primarily to overcome this type of systematic inconsistency in judgement. And important too that we develop ways of dealing with our heuristics. Here are some basic thoughts to help you.

1. Alter the availability heuristic: It is very simple, using the information at the top of our minds, to construct scenarios that lead to success. Practise asking yourself the question "what could happen to change my mind?"

2. Be contrary: Once you have made your decision deliberately attempt to support the opposite view.

3. Reframe the question: Rather than "why shouldn't I lend?" consider "why should I lend?"

4. Perhaps most importantly, develop the habit of trusting base line as opposed to case-specific data. Base-line data is that which has been proven by experience and testing whereas case-specific data relates to only one particular scenario.

    For example, it is well proven that small shops with two or three full-time staff can be profitable. Do not allow a grandly presented business plan with great cash flows and projections delivered by somebody you trust (in the normal course of events) persuade you that a small business can support (or needs) eight full timers.

Using base-line data tends to remove random inconsistencies and is a good systematic consistence to develop.

A final example of base-line as opposed to case-specific data:

> *In Cardiff there are 15 Classics lecturers and 150 long-distance lorry drivers. Jonathon is five foot seven and slim and enjoys poetry and Mozart. Is Jonathon a classics lecturer or a lorry driver?*

Case data and the representational heuristics will lead some people to assume Jonathon is a classics lecturer whereas base-line data suggests he is ten times more likely to be a lorry driver.

We are leaving the Introduction now. As stated in footnote 2, you will not be examined on these theoretical aspects which I have briefly introduced. I felt, however, that it was important to set a basic framework on which to build the rest of the text.

1

THE CANONS OF LENDING

The purpose of lending is to make a profit. I thought it best to get that out of the way straightaway, because some believe that profit is a dirty word or, at best, a necessary evil. On the contrary, if financial institutions did not lend then our society and our individual lifestyles would be radically different. There are very few organizations or individuals who do not use credit in their day-to-day lives. If we can accept the fact that lending is neither inherently bad nor its practitioners somewhat beyond the pale then we can start to look at what makes good lending and good lenders and conversely what makes bad lending (and lenders).

Good lending is, in the final analysis, lending that gets repaid. So by extension good lenders are those whose decisions lead to repaid lending. Simple? Well in essence yes, in practice no. Every lending decision involves in part crystal-ball gazing (never completely reliable) and 20/20 hindsight (usually infallible but always too late). The lending decision-making process involves taking in information, analysing it, making a judgement and implementing that judgement. There has been an argument for many years, still unresolved, over the essence of that process. At the heart of the debate is the question

Is lending an art or a science?

Thirty years ago the answer would have been unequivocally – *art*. The practitioners were deemed to be a breed apart gifted with talents beyond those of normal folk. Since that time, however, the demand for fast, efficient credit judgements has increased beyond imagining. The introduction of charge, then credit, then store cards has meant that more lending and more decisions have needed to be made in an ever-decreasing time. The advent of computer technology has played a part (as it has in all areas of our lives) and now most high-street organizations will issue a store card after completion of a simple form and a telephone call. The simple form is a distillation of what are considered to be essential lending factors that are weighted and scored by a computer on a pre-determined basis. This is an application of *science* – called *credit scoring*, which has no human judgmental input at the point of decision. The relevant scores have already been input into the computer program. Credit scoring has been very successful, over the past two decades, in reducing bad debts incurred by personal borrowers and, since the mid 1990s, it has been increasingly used in business lending (albeit at the less complex end of the sector). We will look at credit scoring in more depth later but I would draw your attention to two points:

1) It has reduced the level of bad debts experienced by lenders in the personal sector

2) It is difficult, if not impossible, to say how many requested loans have been turned down that would have been successfully repaid. These loans that should not have been rejected represent lost profit.

So is the art of lending dead? If it were you would not be following this course of study nor would I have been asked to write this book. If lending were purely a scientific process whose parameters could be observed and measured, no lender would ever make a bad decision and no lender would ever lose any money. However to ignore science and its benefits would serve only to increase bad decisions and bad debts.

Lending is neither art nor science; rather it is an amalgam of both. The most competent lender is like the conductor of an orchestra. He follows the notes as displayed on the musical score but conducts from somewhere within himself. In the same way the business plans, balance sheets and ratios provide the framework and these are analysed by all the tools at our disposal. But the decision we make will often come down to a personal feeling of "I like this project" or "I trust this borrower".

What this text, and the workbook which accompanies it, seeks to do is to introduce you to the tools and thought processes which, if followed, will greatly enhance the quality of your decision making. What will enhance that decision making even more is the experience you will gain as you practise. It is cold comfort to know that you will be a better lender at 56 than at 26. But, however experienced you become, never think that you know all the tricks and possess all the skills. However, at the beginning of your career you are more concerned with how few skills and how little experience you have. An invaluable resource as you study this subject and begin to practise is the body of experienced lenders in your organization. Cultivate them. However, as any experienced lender will tell you, there are *no* foolproof or guaranteed tricks to ensure all loans get repaid. As you start your lending career I can promise you one thing – at some point you will make a decision that will cost your employer money. The good news is that your employer is expecting it and is factoring the cost of it into the price of the loans offered (more of this later). It is highly probable that your decision will have been affirmed by somebody else, but it will have been your decision and you will feel awful. When it happens have a look at the original papers and think about what you might have done differently. When you do this one of three outcomes is possible:

1) You will see absolutely nothing wrong. This will almost certainly be because there **is** nothing wrong with the application, or your decision-making process. The lending did not get repaid because of an external factor outside anybody's control. The sad thing is that in these cases the lender is joined in the loss by the borrower.

2) You will see where you went wrong. The obvious trick here is to learn from your mistake because even the most patient of employers will move you out of lending if you *keep* making the same mistakes.

3) You were conned/hoodwinked/bamboozled. It is unfortunate, but sadly true, that a small number of prospective borrowers will be setting out to defraud you. Remember those rules of thumb for good lending? Here's the first:

Trust your gut instinct – if something, somewhere inside says no then be very, very careful about saying yes.

This does not mean you say no immediately. Talk to a colleague, ask advice, ask for more details from the borrower, and sleep on your decision. Never let anybody rush you. However important the matter is to them you have a different set of obligations.

Primary among these obligations is to those whose money you are lending. Rule of thumb two:

It is not your money.

As you should be aware from your previous studies, the money you are lending belongs to shareholders, depositors and others who have lent to your financial institution.

The best lenders tend to be those who are fully aware that it is not their money they are lending, *but act is if it were.*

1.1   The lending equation

There are several elements within the lending equation.

1) the financial institution:

 a) bank;

 b) building society;

 c) insurance company;

 d) miscellaneous.

Each of these bodies has different goals and aims and often seeks to service the requirements of a particular type of borrower to the exclusion of others. This may be through choice or because of the structure of the institution. You will be aware that the mutual status of building societies limits the level and type of facilities that can be offered to the lucrative corporate business sector. And indeed the restriction on the type and level of services that can be offered by building societies is one reason for the glut of de-mutualizations seen over the last five years.

2) the borrower:

 a) personal;

 i) individuals;

 ii) joint;

 b) business;

 i) sole traders;

 ii) partnerships;

    iii) limited companies;

    iv) public limited companies;

  c) miscellaneous;

    i) clubs/associations;

    ii) trustees and executors;

    iii) charities.

3) The conduit (you):

You are not alone. Even when you have been given your own sanctioning authority you are part of a team. Consider yourself to be the "Loan Arranger" but never the "Lone Ranger". You will develop your own style and techniques but this will take time.

4) *The introducer*: This is a group of professionals who as part of their main business will help/advise borrowers. This group includes (but is not limited to):

  i) accountants;

  ii) solicitors;

  iii) financial advisors.

All the above are good sources of new lending and many employers actively encourage the development of strong links with them. Always remember, however, that each of these groups has a different type of relationship with its clients than you do and that, as a consequence, different sets of priorities exist. Sometimes these priorities are in opposition. It is important that you always maintain an arms-length arrangement with introducers while at the same time maintaining the highest respect for their skills, abilities and integrity.

It is also worth remembering that many (if not most) borrowers will have one or more professional advisors. Although in many ways these are competitors they are not an enemy. An experienced lender will welcome the input of other advisors and seeks always to work with them.

5) The facility will be looked at in depth in Chapter 3 but to summarize very briefly:

  i) overdrafts;

    The overdraft facility is a form of revolving credit.

  ii) personal loans;

  iii) mortgage loans;

  iv) bridging finance.

6) The process: whether it is an art or a science lending is improved by realizing that adopting a methodological approach. This approach can be defined by considering the following basic canons of lending:

Who am I lending to?

What am I lending it for?

Why am I lending it?

When will I get repaid?

How will I get repaid?

How can I check I will/I am getting repaid?

Mnemonics

All the lending organizations have various methods of codifying the above into user-friendly mnemonics. These are *CAMPARI, MARS, PARSER* and *CCCPARTS*.

For the purposes of this text we will concern ourselves primarily with *CAMPARI*, which stands for:

Character

Ability

Margin

Purpose

Amount

Repayment

Insurance

For you to be successful in your lending career (and the exam) you really need to understand this process so here goes!

Character

Throughout the history of both the stock exchange and other financially-orientated organizations such as Lloyd's of London the dictum "My word is my bond" has been the underpinning stanchion whereby business was conducted. Once a gentleman had given his word on a matter to a third party that third party could rely on the performance of the word. Honour would demand no less. A broken word would leave the gentleman both socially and professionally isolated. This system worked for many years. Not because our ancestors were inherently more trustworthy than us but because the business community was so small. As this changed so did the reliance on the dictum. Over the past thirty to forty years the question of "who am I am dealing with?" has become more and more crucial. The best debtor is one who is willing to repay but is having trouble doing so whereas the worst is one who could repay but seeks to avoid the debt.

In any lending situation the crucial question is "Do I trust this person to repay me?" – or to put it another way – "is this a person of good character?" How can we tell?

Unfortunately first impressions count and in this we are hampered by a whole load of mental and emotional baggage. If a person comes in to see us dressed nicely and speaking respectfully we instantly warm to them. We may occasionally find the person physically attractive. Do these factors make them any more trustworthy than the scruffy customer who treats us like a lackey? "Of course not!" you say indignantly "I am far too sophisticated to fall into that trap". Be that as it may, how are you going to decide how trustworthy?

If the potential borrower (applicant) is a customer then the task is a little easier. Some questions that can be asked are:

How long has Mr X been a customer? – A loan request from a customer who opened his account last week would obviously be greeted with a little more wariness than one from a customer of a few months standing. In the past, some organizations have restricted loans to customers of one or two years standing.

Has Mrs Y borrowed before? – This is an excellent guideline. Was the debt repaid on time without problems? Yes? – Go ahead (see later caveats). If the debt was not repaid on time then be very wary.

If the applicant has not borrowed before things are a little more difficult. You can consider whether or not the customer has been a problem before – I am a university lecturer and in any one year will lecture to over 250 individual students. The only names I know with any certainty are the problems. Some customers will impinge themselves on your consciousness for all sorts of reasons. Most notable is the customer who regularly anticipates salary receipt, forcing you to consider bouncing cheques[1].

Generally, however, subjective judgement on trustworthiness can be greatly assisted by use of credit reference agencies[2]. The original credit reference search will be on file and will show any adverse factors. If it is substantially out of date – or if the applicant has moved – it may be prudent to re-search. In the absence of anything detrimental (and subject to the other factors) you should lend. You are still at risk but lending is a risk business. In his excellent book *Against the Gods – the Ultimate Story of Risk*[3], Peter Bernstein states that the word credit derives from the Latin *risicare* meaning, "to dare". Every time you lend you are daring to believe. In essence you are reverting to the art side of the equation . Every lender will tell you that your instinct about character develops over the years.

Before leaving our consideration of character there is one last point. You need to think of character as a reverse trawler's net. If the applicant cannot satisfy you as to their character do not lend. Everything else that follows in the mnemonic is important but nothing is of greater importance than the character of the applicant. On a similar vein nothing is less important than the security. Excellent security does not turn a sow's ear into a silk purse.

Ability

Mainly of use in business propositions, this factor concerns itself with "does the applicant

[1] See anticipatory limits in Chapter 3.
[2] See Chapter 2.
[3] Bernstein published by Wiley 1996 ISBN 0471121045.

have the necessary skills and abilities to accomplish what is proposed"?

Dentists are great with teeth – highly skilled and trained – but as heart surgeons? I think not. Well not for me anyway.

When considering a proposal it is essential that you identify what abilities will be needed to succeed and to seek from the applicant evidence that he or she processes them all. Acceptable evidence would be relevant educational qualifications and/or experience in the proposed area. Allied to the skills needed for the proposed project is "does the applicant have the business skills to succeed"? This is not to say that the applicant needs to be an accountant, or a lawyer or a marketing genius but there needs to be evidence of an understanding of basic book keeping skills, etc. In many instances with sole traders and small partnerships there may be ample evidence of extreme competency within the applicant's specialized field but little or no evidence of business skills. Is this a reason not to lend? No – it is an opportunity to help a business to succeed by introducing them to your bank's small business advisor who will be able to supply the skills the business lacks.

Having decided that the business needs skills A through to G how can the applicant prove that he or she possesses them? The most usual method is via a simple CV. As proposals become more complex (and for larger amounts) the applicant will (should) supply a business plan. This will, if prepared properly, identify the skills needed and give evidence of their existence within the business. In large cases, and in start-up situations, the lack of a business plan[4] is a clear alarm bell that the business lacks the necessary skills.

Do not expect to find all the skills in one person (even *you* are not that good). It would be perfectly acceptable, and encouraging, for an applicant to present the proposal based on his or her talents and to inform you that a bookkeeper or accountant is employed to assist on the business side. Why is this encouraging? Well it shows that the borrower has a realistic view of his or her own strengths and weakness and acts accordingly.

Margin

This is the price of the facility. In many instances it will be centrally set, e.g.:

- personal overdrafts;
- personal loans;
- house mortgages;
- credit cards.

In these cases the lending office will have no authority to set a different margin. However, in the majority of business lending the margin will be set to reflect the level of risk you, the lender, feel you are at.

In general, margins are expressed as X% above base rate. For large corporate lending the base rate may be replaced by London Inter-Bank Offered Rate (LIBOR) and X will be expressed in basis points (100 basis points equals one per cent). Into X central management

---

[4] Or the well-known "back of an envelope job".

will have added a weighting for, amongst other things, bad debts, other expenses and profit.

Many organizations set a preliminary X at 3% or 3.5%, and this is varied according to the overall deal.

1) Is the client undoubted?

2) Is the proposal a sure-fire success?

3) What is the level of the loan compared with the client's stake?

4) Is there good security?

5) Is there intense competition for this client?

If you were considering two proposals on the same day and client A answers yes to all five of the above question and client B answers yes to only (1) and (4) is it not equitable that client A has a lower rate? (The phrase finer rate is often used.)

The complicating factor is that both client A and client B believe that they deserve a finer rate than you want to charge. In many cases setting the margin will be a process of negotiation between you and the client. It is, therefore, sometimes a good idea to state that the rate is 4.0% and let the client negotiate you down to 3.5%. If he or she accepts 4.0% you have gained an extra 0.5% interest.

A word of caution – never get so caught up in the negotiation that you find yourself offering a lower rate than your assessment of the risk.

Two more questions arise. Is there a minimum percentage above base rate? In practice no – some large companies have some very fine rates. In ordinary lending it would be rare to see a rate lower than 2% above base rate. On the other hand is there a higher rate above which it is unwise to go?. Despite the rates charged on some credit cards in relation to base rate the practical answer must be yes. Anything above 5.5-6.0% is very risky business. Any customer willing to pay 6 % over base must be very desperate. Although you might wish to consider the rates on some credit and store cards.

Purpose

There are a limitless number of purposes that could be presented to a lender. However they fall broadly into the following categories:

1) *Liquidity.* Many people and businesses experience times when the short-term outflow of funds exceeds the short-term influx.

2) *Asset purchase.* These are normally medium- to long-term situations such as the purchase of new plant and machinery by a business or a new car or house by personal borrowers.

3) *Business start-up or buy-out.* Many of the requests received will be from individuals wishing to start their own business or buy into an existing one. In each of these cases a business plan is a necessity.

The two most important aspects with regards to purpose are for the lender to ensure that the purpose is proper, i.e. that it lawful and moral, and that it is realistic. Many borrowers (especially business borrowers) are overoptimistic and care must be exercised by the lender to prevent this optimism from spreading.

Amount

The amount borrowed is of course important in financial terms. However, several factors must be borne in mind by the lender.

Firstly, how has the amount borrowed been arrived at by the applicant? Evidence of the level of need and the underlying assumptions are vital. In most cases the amount will be linked either to cash-flow forecasts or to the proposed purchase price of an asset.

Second, a lender needs to consider the appropriateness of the amount – is it sufficient? Is the requested amount too much? It is better to carefully examine a cash flow and decide that the overdraft facility needs to be £30,000 as opposed to a request for £25,000.

Finally the customer's stake needs to be considered. How much is he or she providing? This might be evidenced by the level of owner's capital within a business or by the amount of deposit being put down towards an asset purchase.

During the great property slump of the late 1980s and early 1990s there was proliferation of 100% mortgages offered together with the added incentive of all costs added to the loan. This meant that in many thousands of cases the borrower owed more than the value of the asset. This is called negative equity and sadly for many this ended in tears with thousands of people losing their homes as interest rates rose to record levels.

Nor was this confined to the personal borrowing sector. Many lenders lent vast sums *secure* in the knowledge that rising property prices protected them from losses. They were proved wrong.

The phenomenon of negative equity has now largely passed and hopefully the lessons have been learnt by both lenders and borrowers.

In most cases, now, all lenders will be looking for prospective borrowers to be inputting some of their own funds. This may be as low as 5% for a house purchase rising to a third where a business is acquiring property.

Repayment

The key questions here are simple – What is the source of repayment and when will repayment be made?

There are several possible sources for repayment. In the personal sector the primary source will be the salary (salaries) of the borrowers or, occasionally, the sale of assets such as shares. It is therefore prudent to have each personal borrower complete a budget planner to show evidence of surplus monies each month from which repayments can be made. Your employer will certainly have such a planner incorporated into its personal loan application forms. If you have never completed one, can I suggest you do so now before reading on.

Having completed the planner let me ask a question – "How come you have so much month left at the end of the money?" According to your calculations on the planner you should be better off than you know you are. This is usual and should be remembered whenever you consider a customer's budget planner. We all underestimate our expenditure. This does not mean that you send it back to the applicant with a note saying "Don't believe you. Try again". Consider instead a more subtle approach. If the planner shows that the applicant has £250 per month spare every month, has he or she missed out anything obvious – such as electricity or rates? A common omission is the cost of the annual holiday. Are there any aspects that are obviously wrong? For example, a couple might estimate that they spend £50 per week on food – is this realistic? Is the expenditure added up correctly?

The second part of this approach would be to ask yourself "If the client has a £250 per month surplus where is the last six months surplus?" If there were a £250 per month surplus there should be about £1,500 credit on the account or in some other form of asset.

It would be foolish indeed to agree to a facility whose cost was equal to the surplus calculated on the budget planner. Your own organization may very well have its own internal rules permitting a facility cost equivalent to 50-60% of the surplus.

For a business the repayment will be coming from profits and we will be examining business accounts and the assessment thereof later.

Insurance

There are now two aspects to this part of the mnemonic.

Historically the *insurance* was a euphemism for security and as such was viewed as the fallback position by a lender. If repayments were not made from the expected sources the lender would realize[5] the security to repay the outstanding debt. The borrower would then have forfeited the asset pledged as security if the borrowing was not repaid.

There is a world of difference in taking security as a lender and the seemingly similar scenario of pawnbroking. In the latter an asset is left in the care of a lender for an agreed period and money advanced against the value. At the end of the agreed period the borrower repays the debt (plus charges) and retrieve the asset. The lender is comfortable because he or she can sell the asset to recoup the outlay. Repayment is secure as the amount advanced will be far lower than the actual market value of the asset.

Taking security is different. The lender who needs to realize the security has a problem. It means that the lending process has failed. Perhaps the facility should never have been granted or perhaps factors outside the borrower's control have led to failure.

A good lender will *never* lend because the proposition includes good security. If the proposal does not make good business sense without security, existence of security does not make it a good proposal. Good security does not make a sow's ear into a silk purse. So why bother

---

[5] Generally this means sell or otherwise turn into cash.

with it? Good question. If every borrower were completely undoubted and every proposition guaranteed to succeed then there would be no need. But the business environment is a risk environment and while risk can be minimized by careful planning and hard work, it cannot be eliminated from a situation.

As previously stated, some businesses will fail for reasons outside the control of both the borrower and lender. The taking of security is a mechanism for ensuring that all parties share in the pain.

In truth the taking of security is the lender's method of minimizing the pain the lender experiences because it must be remembered that all lenders are lending not their own funds but those of their depositors and investors. Any bad debts reduce the potential returns to them.

Does this mean that all borrowing should be secured? By no means, and the majority of short- and medium-term personal borrowing is unsecured. There are several reasons for this:

1. Most borrowing of this nature is small in real monetary terms.

2. The interest rates (margins) seen in this type of borrowing are very high and what losses there are can be recouped from the interest earned from the good loans.

3. The growth of sophisticated credit-scoring systems has reduced the numbers of bad debts.

4. The risks of external factors causing non-repayment are much less. In most personal borrowing, repayment comes from a regular salary and the main dangers to this source are easy to identify – redundancy and illness preventing the earning of a salary. Not only are these dangers identifiable they are also, to some extent, quantifiable. This makes them insurable. Many insurance companies offer the following policies:

    Accident, Sickness and Redundancy – a general insurance policy which, in return for a small premium, covers a borrower against the three named risks. Some pay an agreed lump sum, others an income for a period of two years.

    Permanent Health Insurance – a life insurance policy that pays up to 66% of a claimant's gross income if he or she is unable to work due to serious health impairment.

If the borrower decides to take up these insurances then the facility is in fact, if not in name, secured. Have a look at your employer's loan application forms. Are there any which *do not* offer one or other of these policies?

The question of security is far more important in the area of business lending. The amounts are generally higher and the margins much finer. The reasons for business failures are far too many to list and quantify and thus impossible to insure. For example, it is not possible for a business to insure against falling sales or stock obsolescence. Some areas, such as non-payment by debtors, can be protected and we will consider some of those later.

The major reason for taking security is to *tie* the borrower into the debt. Consider the situation were a business has been set up with £10,000 worth of capital injected by the owner. A lender provides an overdraft facility of £25,000 based on projections supplied by the owner. What happens if the overdraft stands at £24,999 and the borrower says that the business cannot succeed? And further that he is emigrating to start a new life in Outer Mongolia? The customer will have lost his £10,000 (unless part of the £24,999 has repaid him that) but the bank has lost £25,000. If the lender has no security he has no option but to sue the borrower through the courts to get him to honour the debt. This is time-consuming, expensive and not certain to succeed. If, however, the lender had security belonging to the borrower that it could sell to reduce or eliminate the debt, would the borrower quit so precipitously? The theory says no. And so, in most business situations, some form of security will be taken. We will look in greater depth at security in Chapter 6.

The mnemonic CAMPARI is, as already stated, popularly used. However the following table gives details of the other popular aids:

Table 1.1: Mnemonics

MARS	PARSER	CCCPARTS
Man	**P**rincipal	**C**ommitment
Amount	**A**mount	**C**haracter
Repayment	**R**epayment	**C**apability
Security	**S**ecurity	**P**urpose
	Expediency	**A**mount
	Repayment	**R**epayment
		Terms
		Security

It is worth looking at expediency and remuneration before leaving our consideration of lending techniques.

Expediency – Lending because it is the prudent course of action. Specifically this usually means lending even if the risk appears great because not to lend might have worse consequences. For example, the out-of-work offspring of one of your best customers asks for an increase in his or her overdraft facility. While every conventional test might be failed and lending normally denied, you might well decide that the possible loss of a few hundred pounds is better than risking offending the parent and losing a major customer who generates £100,000 p.a. interest for your branch. The major problem here is that, because of your duty of confidentiality to your customer (the offspring), you cannot approach the parent (your customer) and talk about the child's finances. It may well be that the lending does go bad and the parent says "hard luck".

Remuneration – You should bear in mind that there are several ways of earning from the customer:

Interest: The majority of the earnings will normally come from the interest earned on the overdraft or loan.

Commission: In many cases it is possible to generate one-off payments via facility fees (often called arrangement fees). And of course commission will be earned from the turnover charge on the current account.

Extras: Most financial institutions now target employees in relation to the selling of other, non-lending products. These will often be life insurance products which generate a fee related to the premium. We will look at the various types of life insurance policies and their uses as security in Chapter 6.

1.2   Practical applications

It is probably a good idea to work through a few examples. Using actual CIB and CIB-style questions we will work through three personal lending scenarios. They will all follow the same format. The question will be shown in italics but we will discuss each section individually.

Example 1: Mr Jakes

Mr John Jakes has banked with you for four years. In recent months you have noticed a tendency for him to anticipate his salary (which averages £1,300 per month). Yesterday you received a telephone call from Mr Jakes and you have arranged an appointment with him for today.

Points to note and consider.

This a sole account. As far as you know Mr Jakes is a single man. It would be prudent to look back at the account opening form and find out what Mr Jakes does for a living. You can also see if there were any adverse credit reference indications. The sentence *"In recent months you have noticed a tendency for Mr Jakes to anticipate his salary"* leads to the consideration – is there an anticipatory limit on this account? Very probably. If so what level and is that being breached? (probably not or you would have written to him). Other useful questions to consider: Does Mr Jakes have a cheque guaranteed card? (what limit?). Has he been issued with the bank's credit card? Again what limit? Has he borrowed from us before – what for? – when repaid?

The fact that he telephoned you (and not the other way round) suggests that the overdraft is within its anticipatory limit – more of this in Chapter 3. His proactiveness is a good point. It would be useful to look at the customer file to see if this situation has happened before. Also ask colleagues if they have any knowledge of the customer. If nothing else you will have a better picture of him for the meeting.

In preparation for the meeting you have examined Mr Jakes' account and noticed the following regular monthly payments.

	£
Building society	*400*
Hire purchase	*250*
TV rental	*30*
Clothing retailer	*50*
Council tax	*100*

The account is currently £320 overdrawn and there is a cheque in clearing for £80 in favour of your bank's credit card company. Mr Jakes' salary is due within the next few days.

"You have examined Mr Jakes' account". The obvious starting point but what are you looking for?

1) The regular payments outlined above. (*Note:* these can be standing orders or direct debits.)

   The regular payments are useful not only for what they include but also what isn't included. The total amount of regular bills budgeted for is £830 but there are none of the following which could reasonably be expected:

   Gas

   Electricity

   Car insurance

   Water rates

   Telephone

   Insurance policy payments

   Are there others that YOU regularly pay?

   Mr Jakes has an income of £1,300 per month and shown expenditure of £830 leaving £470 for the gas, etc. and general living expenses. Obviously you will want to know from Mr Jakes how he pays for these other regular expenses.

2) The closing position before the salary is received: when accounts get under pressure the closing balance gets closer and closer to the overdraft limit. If we assume the anticipatory limit is £650 (half the average salary) then closing balances over the last few months of:

M1	150 od
M2	215 od

| M3 | 275 od |
| Current month | 400 od (320 + 80) |

would be cause for concern. It suggests very strongly that Mr Jakes is living beyond his means and would in two to three months be breaching his anticipatory limit.

3) The number of cheques written – especially round amounts. Consider most of the goods we purchase. They are normally £X.99 or £X.49. The items we mainly pay for in round figures are petrol (does Mr Jakes have a car?) and credit card debts.

4) The numbers of payments received into the account. Generally there would just be the salary. Are other amounts paid in? When? From what source? If there are cheques paid in towards the end of the month could Mr Jakes have another account somewhere else? Are these receipts followed a few days later by equal amounts paid out? Is Mr Jakes crossfiring[6]?

Do you have a picture in your head of Mr Jakes? Is he a single man living the high life on the bank's money? Drives a flashy car perhaps?

At your meeting Mr Jakes apologises for the overdrawn balance . He explains that he went on holiday with his wife and two children (aged 9 and 12) a couple of months ago and it cost more than he had expected. Consequently, from a financial point of view, he was recovering slowly.

Sorry to disappoint you but there are several good points that begin to emerge in Mr Jakes' favour.

1) He apologises – a starter for 10. Sincerity would need to be judged (back to art).

2) He explains – we now know the *purpose* behind the debt.

3) He is a family man – not always a good point but family men tend to be more stable and likely to repay.

4) He acknowledges the continuing problem.

5) He has a solution – he has thought about the situation.

The main questions here are – How much did the holiday cost? and How was it paid for? Savings or credit card?

During your discussion the following points emerge:

a) *Mr Jakes changed house 15 months ago. The property cost £70,000 and the mortgage is £34,000.*

b) *A new car was purchase a year ago with the help of a three-year HP deal.*

c) *Mrs Jakes works part-time and receives £40 per week in cash. Hence Mr Jakes only contributes £200 per month for housekeeping expenses.*

d) *Tax and insurance on the car is now due amounting to £240.*

[6] A process which involves feeding one bank account with funds from another in a circular pattern with insufficient funds to cover the payments.

e) *He also has a pressing bill for house repairs amounting to £240.*

f) *Mr Jakes is due to receive a salary increase of 3% in two months' time.*

Questions arising from the above:

1) Given his salary (which grossed out to about £23,000) why did he take such a small mortgage? Is it in joint names? – do not assume it is just because he is married. He does not have a joint account, does he? Who is the mortgage with? What type of mortgage is it? Is the interest rate fixed, capped or variable? Does the £400 include the life insurance and the buildings and contents insurance? Did the equity come from the sale of a previous house or savings or a gift/inheritance?

2) What was this brand new car? What did it cost? Did he put anything in part exchange? How much did he borrow from the HP company? Does he intend to change the car soon?

3) Does Mrs Jakes have a bank account? Where? The £200 housekeeping takes the disposable income from £470 to £270 pm.

4) Tax and insurance amount to £20 p.m. if budgeted for. Taking disposable income down further to £250 pm.

5) Pressing. Hmmm… What does *pressing* mean? Who is pressing? Why has Mr Jakes not paid by credit card? Proper budgeting should allow for this type of expense.

6) He is due an increase of 3%. This will equate to £39 pm net.

We can now construct a partial budget for Mr Jakes:

Income	1339
Less regular expenses	830
Food	200
Tax and insurance	20
Emergency	<u>30</u>
	259 to cover
Gas	
Electricity	
Water rates	
Telephone	

At this point Mr Jakes should be able to tell us how these are funded. It may be (probably is) out of his wife's £40 per week. If it is not, i.e all her income[7] goes on food and clothes,

---

[7] Don't forget this will include approximately £75 p.m. child benefit.

etc., then Mr Jakes could have a disposable income as low as £60 pm.

Mr Jakes must also tell us the balance on the credit card. £80 could be a complete repayment or at a minimum payment of 5% representing £1,600. Note that some cards have minimum repayments of 3% taking the debt to £2,400. We definitely need to know the outstanding balance. We could also ask if the couple has any savings.

Mr Jakes asks for a loan of £2,000 repayable at £75 per month. Giving reasons, explain how you would respond to this request.

The nub of the question. Before we can answer it we need to ask a few more questions.

We know the overdraft is £400 with a few days to go until salary. Let's say £500.

The tax, insurance and repair bill come to £480. Round up to £500. This gives total debts of £1000. So linking this into the P and the A from CAMPARI what does he want the extra £1000 for? The most likely scenario, which covers a few of the holes above, is that the holiday was paid for on the credit card and the amount outstanding is approximately £1,000. If we take the figure of £2,000 as needed then where does the £75 p.m. come from? – Answer: Our loan repayment tables which he will have undoubtedly looked at before coming into see us[8]. So what period is he asking for the loan over. The figures suggest three years.

So, in essence, we are being asked to grant a three-year, unsecured personal loan to pay for a holiday (already taken), the cost of which is currently on a credit card and on overdraft. The £75 cost of the loan would be a little less than the credit card payment.

OK. Spend a few minutes on your own applying CAMPARI then compare with my thoughts.

Character	We know nothing detrimental about him. He came to us with his problem and apologised.
Ability	He has a well-paid job. He does seem a little financially naïve and certainly could do with some advice on budgeting.
Margin	Rates for personal loans set by head office.
Purpose	Holiday.
Amount	£2000.
Repaymentability	From salary – net disposable income £250 (call it £200). Cost of loan £75 pm leaving £125.
Insurance	Unsecured but equity in property.

I would say yes.

Character is good. Married man with two children in what appears to be long-term, well-paid job. (Do another credit reference.) The purpose is acceptable (although I would have preferred to have been asked in advance). The amount is small. Repayment is a little tight.

[8] We are not the only people to prepare for interviews; customers often come prepared.

If his wife were not paying the gas, etc. the answer would be no. Insurance – insist on payment protection.

To enable monitoring I would remove or reduce the anticipatory limit to about £100.

If Mrs Jakes is not paying the utilities bills then we are looking at a disposable income of about £60 pm and a different situation altogether. How might we approach that?

If we say no Mr Jakes will try and get the loan elsewhere (and succeed). This means we lose this loan and all future loans he might apply for. We may even lose the current account.

In the worst-case scenario we have a couple who in the last 15 months have:

- bought a new house;
- bought a new car;
- been on an expensive holiday.

and consequently have severe cash flow problems. Obviously the main pressure is the £250 payable to the HP company and the credit-card debt.

What if we remortgaged the house and took out the HP and Credit Card and overdraft etc.?

The HP is at about £6,000[9] and the requested loan £2,000. This £8,000 would be at house mortgage loan rates (say 8%), which means a monthly payment of:

£75 (including capital repayments)

This makes the couple £250 per month better off and effectively solvent. The downside is they are buying the car over a longer period.

From the bank's point of view we are now lending £42,000 secured against a property valued at £70,000 and will pick up the buildings and contents insurance.

The customer would be happy and we would monitor the account very closely for twelve months or so.

Example 2: Mr And Mrs Stevens

Mr and Mrs Stevens have banked with you for over twenty years. Mr Stevens is a school teacher (aged 55) and Mrs Stevens (aged 49) has been a chef at a local restaurant for the past nine years. They have no children. Their salaries are £25,000 and £12,000, respectively. They telephone to arrange a meeting "to discuss a business proposal." Prior to the meeting you ascertain the following facts:

The information to hand is encouraging. This is a long-standing account and both customers are employed in long-term careers. They have a joint income of £37,000, which would suggest that there should be some (substantial?) savings. The absence of savings given their ages and income (and no children) would be a concern.

---

[9] Three-year agreement minus one year equals two years: twenty-four payments of £250.

They have several accounts with you:

Joint Current account	*1500.00 Cr.*	*Limit 500*
Mr Stevens C/A	*375.48 Cr.*	*Limit 500*
Mrs Stevens C/A	*489.21 Cr.*	*Limit 500*
Mortgage Account	*5800.89 Dr.*	*Limit 6000*
Deposit Account	*2500.00 Cr.*	

They have just finished repaying a personal loan of £7,500 granted five years ago, which was used to fund a car purchase.

Their joint account has direct debits and standing orders set up for all the regular expenses and the regular monthly outgoings come to £975 pm. The joint account is fed by a standing order of £800 from Mr Stevens and £400 from Mrs Stevens.

The information just gets better and better. The current accounts are in credit (although you would look at the swings and average balances on the accounts) and the mortgage account nearly repaid. The £2,500 on deposit shows a propensity to save although you perhaps expected more. In all probability there are other accounts with other financial institutions and an investigation of direct debits would reveal the overall level of savings in endowments, unit trusts, etc.

They appear to budget carefully as the monthly payments into the bills account (joint) exceed the regular payments – this has built up a buffer for unexpected expenses.

The repayment of the personal loan is another excellent sign. The best borrower is a second- and third-time borrower. You could even look at the accounts to see what the monthly repayments were. If the request is for another £7,500 to change the car again the answer is yes straightaway.

You may want to ask yourself what is the value of the house now. This can, at this stage, be achieved either from your own local knowledge of the area where they live or from a colleague.

At the meeting they advise you that Mr Stevens has been offered early retirement, which will involve an annual pension[10] of £8,400 p.a. and a lump sum of £24,000. They have decided to accept the offer and purchase a small restaurant that they have been thinking about for a few years. It is on the market for £85,000. They tell you that they intend funding the purchase as follows:

	£
Purchase price	*85,000*
Own cash	*50,000*
Shortfall	*35000*

And they ask for the bank's assistance by way of a loan of £35,000.

---

[10] Assume teaching for 23 years + 6 years enhancement in an 80th's scheme.

Give reasons how do you respond to this request?

Let us jump straight into CAMPARI.

Character

We are really comfortable here. Long-standing customers who have been borrowing from us for years and have repaid at least one personal loan.

Ability

We know that they can manage their own finances in an exemplary manner. But can they run a restaurant?

The evidence in the question suggests yes. Mrs Stevens has been chef for many years. Their proven financial acumen in their personal affairs bodes well but we would want to investigate this area a little more. (Possible referral to small business banker?)

Margin

Never decide this third. Having M here makes the mnemonic work but this does not form part of the decision-making process – you consider the rate after deciding to lend.

Purpose

To purchase an existing business. Always an acceptable purpose providing that the price is right and the business is sound. The problem here is that Mr and Mrs Stevens appear to have brought no details of the business. There are three sets of details they might have brought.

a)   The particulars prepared by the business transfer agency[11]. This will contain details of the location of the business, an outline of the type of business and brief (very brief) indications of turnover, and the asking price. As with all details of this type these are an opening gambit. Nobody pays the asking price and nobody relies on turnover figures, etc. They normally take up one or two sides of A4 paper and will usually contain a picture. Have a look in your local evening paper and send for one. Note that for this type of business stock will be an extra cost.

b)   A business valuation report is an independent, in-depth report on the business, its history, its performance and its prospects. The advantage is that it will be able to say whether the restaurant is performing as well as the *average* restaurant of similar size and type. These reports can be expensive.

c)   The accounts. Obviously these will need to be seen and for at least three years. They will give some indication of the level of goodwill the purchaser is being asked to pay. In general terms this will be the difference between the net asset value and the sale price.

Amount

Is £35,000 sufficient?

[11] Like an estate agent but for businesses – widely used.

On the face of things yes, but the Stevenses have forgotten three important extras.

Firstly no allowance has been made for legal and survey costs. These could be as high as £2,000. This makes the requested loan £37,000 rather than £35,000.

You should also note at this point that the customers are putting down £50,000. This is £26,000 more than the pension lump sum. Where is this coming from? The possible sources are:

● *Other savings and investments* – query how much they will have left after the deposit.

● *Sale of their domestic property* – it is possible that the restaurant has living accommodation attached. You would want to ascertain the net cash position of the couple after selling their current house and repaying the mortgage and putting the £50,000 down. Secondly the customers have neglected to account for the stock which will be sold at valuation. For a restaurant this may not be substantial but for businesses such as a corner shop, newsagents, ironmongers, etc. the stock valuation could be high.

Finally and most importantly the couple do not appear to have considered the need for an overdraft facility. Any new business will require time to get on its feet and to generate sales and thus cash flow. The suppliers of the restaurant might initially be reluctant to extend credit to people unknown to them. It would be normal in this circumstance for the request to include an "in case of need" overdraft facility.

Repayment

Where is repayment coming from? The key to remember is that both Mr and Mrs Stevens are giving up their jobs and that the only guaranteed income will be from a pension.

A loan of £37,000 over 10 years would cost between £5,500 and £8,000 (depending on base rate and margin). So obviously the income generated by the business is going to be vital and we will need evidence of this.

In some ways this deal would be more comfortable if Mr Stevens were keeping his job (and his £23,000 salary) and we were lending £50,000.

Insurance

The level of security depends on how the purchase price is made up: For example.

	A	B	C
Freehold building	55000	25000	00000
Fixtures and fittings	5000	5000	5000
	60000	30000	5000
Goodwill	25000	55000	80000
Purchase price	85000	85000	85000

Scenarios A and B give us real security (from the freehold building) but scenario C gives none.

However this level of loan facility would require some form of security and there is the matrimonial home, which has a very small mortgage and which we already have a charge over. What is that worth? Even a property worth a modest £60,000 gives security value of £45,000 (at 75%).

We have three possible decisions here:

1. We can say yes on the grounds that we have known the couple for many years and we have probably got more than enough security for the loan with the matrimonial home.

2. We can turn the deal down

3. We can agree in principle subject to a number of conditions:

   - we see the accounts

   - we have an independent business valuation carried out.

Choice 1 is called pawnbroking. In this case we have no concern whether or not the business succeeds or fails. If it succeeds we earn our interest. If it fails we realize our security.

Choice 2 is perhaps the easiest option. On the grounds that the Stevenses may be being very foolish giving up to two good jobs and security for an apparently unproven business and we are not pawnbrokers.

Choice 3 is the best. It recognizes the existing skills and abilities of the Stevenses. It makes no judgement on the wisdom of entering business at this stage in their lives. It shows that we value their custom. And by asking for more information it shows that we are concerned about the viability of the project which will affect them more than us.

Always remember that you have the above three decisions available to you at all times. Do not be rushed into a hasty yes or no because the customer is in a rush. For example, if the couple had visited you saying that they were going to bid at auction for the restaurant that afternoon your answer would have to be no.

To complete the story let us assume that the couple return a few days later with the accounts of the restaurant for the three years that it has been open.

Table 1.1

Allstar Restaurant: Trading, Profit and Loss Account for the year ended 31 December 199X

		This Year		Last Year		Year Before
£s						
Sales		158,523		135,888		100,250
Cost of sales		75,222		62,589		50,021
Gross profit		83,301		73,299		50,229
Expenses						
Light/Heat	1,000		859		752	
Lease	12,000		12,000		12,000	
Rates	850		750		650	
Wages	30,000		29,000		28,000	
Depreciation	5,000		5,000		5,000	
Advertising	1,200		900		700	
Professional fees	350		250		250	
		50,400		48,759		47,352
NET PROFIT		32,901		24,540		2,877
Gross profit margin (%)		52.55		53.94		50.10
Net profit margin (%)		20.75		18.06		2.80

Table 1.2: Balance sheet for Allstar Restaurant as at 31 December 199X

£s	This year		Last Year		Year Before	
Fixed Assets						
Leasehold shop	25,000		25,000		25,000	
Fixtures and fittings[12]	25,000		18,000		15,000	
Total fixed assets		50,000		43,000		40,000
Current assets						
Stock	2,000		1,000		800	
Cash	1,500		800		500	
Bank	11,000	14,500	8,000	9,800	5,122	6,422
Current Liabilities						
Trade creditors	1,000	- 1,000	1,000	- 1,000	1,000	-1,000
Working capital[13]		13,500		8,800		5,422
TOTAL NET ASSETS		63,500		51,800		45,422

Mr and Mrs Stevens also advise us of the following facts:

- *As they will be both working in the restaurant the wages bill will be cut by half .*
- *The freeholder has verbally agreed that at the next rent review, due next year, they will looking for an increase in rent to £18,000 p.a..*
- *The current supplier knows Mrs Stevens and is willing to allow the new owners credit on the same basis as the old.*

They will remain in their current house which is they mention is valued at £125,000.

A quick appraisal of the accounts shows that:

- profits have improved every year since inception;
- cash is retained in the business – thus very little need of an overdraft;
- the margins have improved and are reasonable for this type of business;
- there is a leasehold shop which may, dependent on the length remaining on the lease, have some value;
- repaymentability seems probable.

This can be seen by reconstructing the most recent profit and loss figures incorporating the information now to hand.

---

[12] Written down value = cost less accumulated depreciation. If you do not know the phrase it is explained in Chapter 4.
[13] Total current assets less current liabilities.

199X	
Net profit	32901
add back savings in wages	15000
deduct proposed rent increase	− 6000
add in depreciation[14]	5000
Total available	46901
estimated loan cost	6000
available to customers	40901

On the basis of this information we would be pleased to lend £37,000 to Mr and Mrs Stevens over ten years at 3.5% above base rate. The facility would be secured by a new charge over the leasehold of the restaurant – whatever its value.

Note that we have made no judgement as to the fairness, or otherwise, of paying £85,000 for a business whose total fixed assets are £50,000. The difference is goodwill. In this case the goodwill is very similar to the net profit for 199X. If the restaurant fails under the ownership of the Stevenses this *value* disappears. Do some research. Ask some senior colleagues what level of goodwill they would expect to see for this *type* of business. If they say more or less than the equivalent of last year's profit recalculate the purchase price and deal on those figures. Leave the Stevenses' contribution the same.

Example 3: Miss Jenna Parry

Your customer, Miss Jenna Parry, has made an appointment to see you to request a loan of £750 to enable the purchase of a car costing £750. You have never met Miss Parry and prior to the appointment you review everything known about her. The account-opening card reveals that she is 21 years old and has recently graduated with a first-class honours degree in history. The account was opened three months ago with what seems to be a salary credit of £750. This credit has been made on the 28th of every month since. Her account has shown the following closing balances for the three months:

£	
Month 1	550.25 Cr.
Month 2	410.32 Cr.
Month 3	251.66 Cr.

And the current balance (with twelve days until payday) is £280.67 Cr.

You meet Miss Parry and she is charming and polite. She explains that a car will help her to get to and from work far more easily and that she can well afford repayments spread over three years.

---

[14] A non-cash item. See Chapter 4 if you are not sure.

What do you do?

Character

- *You do not know Miss Parry;*
- *she is 21 years old;*
- *The account was opened three months ago.*

This is not encouraging. A loan request after less than six months should always be viewed cautiously. A valid question would be "who were her previous bankers?". People who graduate from university would normally have had a current account for three years. Given the way higher education is funded most students have large overdrafts on graduation. Why did Miss Parry leave her previous bankers? This is always a valid question for any new (newish) customer.

Ability

- *first class honours degree in history*

No doubt as to her academic ability and this suggest that a good career may be ahead. What does Miss Parry do now?

Purpose

- *purchase of a car*

A perfectly acceptable purpose.

Amount

- *£750 for asset costing £750*

This is a major concern. The customer should have some stake in the proposed purchase.

Margin

- Personal loan rates fixed centrally.

Repayment

- *From salary of £750*

Obviously a budget would be required but on the face of things it does not look good. Notice that every month the closing balance is reducing. Miss Parry is obviously overspending. This might be because of one-off costs associated with the new job.

The loan would cost approximately £69 p.m. over one year or £37.50 p.m. over two years. Consider also the following points:

1. A car costing £750 will probably have high maintenance costs.

2. It will probably need replacing within two years.

Insurance

- The car is not suitable for security

- Accident sickness redundancy cover might not be available because Miss Parry has been employed for only three/four months.

Given the above it is highly unlikely that the request will be granted. Miss Parry should be invited to reapply in six months.

Had Miss Parry held her student account with us for three years the decision would probably be yes based on the knowledge gained from how she had conducted her student account.

For most personal lending we will not actually go through the process of interviewing and in-depth consideration. Most financial organizations will utilize credit scoring – which was mentioned earlier in the chapter.

At its simplest credit scoring is a means of applying a numerical score to the various pieces of information garnered from the customer.

Research time – go and pick up one of your institution's personal loan forms. Go and get competitors'. Apart from the style and colour what differences are there?

Most loan application forms are actually based on CAMPARI (or a variant thereof).

A very simple credit scoring system might look like this:

C	100	points
A	100	points
M	100	points
P	100	points
A	100	points
R	100	points
I	100	points
Total	700	points
Pass	More than 351	
Refer to Lending Officer 281 – 350		

In these circumstances the lending officer will look at the information and see what has caused the low score. Has the customer missed out on valuable marks because he or she has just moved house having previously been in the same home for many years?

Decline   less than 280

As previously mentioned it is certain that some (but how many?) applicants scoring less than 280 would have proved to be creditworthy.

The major danger in this system is that there is no element of discrimination. Insurance is given as much weight as character. Can this be right? Obviously not.

A more sophisticated system might be:

C	250	points
A	100	points
M	nil	points
P	50	points
A	50	points
R	200	points
I	50	points
Total	700	points
Pass	More than 351	
Refer to Lending Officer	281 – 350	
Decline	less than 280	

This is more appropriate as it attempts to recognize, in a quantitative manner, the unarguable fact that some elements of CAMPARI are more important than others.

Each system will then be further subdivided and points allocated according to perceived importance. As you examine the application forms you have acquired consider the questions:

1   " How long have you lived there?" and

2   " How long have you banked with us?"

How would you weight these two questions against each other?

Credit-scoring design is complex and based on the large data banks that have been collated by lenders over the years.

You will not be asked to construct a credit scoring system in the exam.

This chapter would not be complete without a brief mention of the Consumer Credit Act 1974. This Act sets out the duties and responsibilities of both the lender (called the creditor in the Act) and the borrower (the debtor). It was enacted to provide protection for personal borrowers from being exploited by unscrupulous lenders. The main facts to bear in mind are:

- it covers only personal (non-corporate) borrowings;
- it covers amounts only up to £25,000;
- it imposes on the lender the duty of clearing showing the annual percentage rate (APR).

This is a reflection of the overall cost of the loan/facility including interest, charges and other costs.

This enables comparison between lenders to be more straightforward for potential customers;

- it builds in a cooling-off period for customers who sign the loan forms away from the lender's premises;

- a cooling-off period is always applied if the loan is secured.

2

CUSTOMERS

In this chapter we will look at the different borrowers and their different legal positions. We will initially consider their different characteristics and needs. The various facilities offered to meet these needs will be covered in depth. The best way to start is to examine the similarities, as once we have examined these we can consider the differences. The greatest area of similarity is in the motivation of customers.

Categories

All customers fall into one of three categories:

Firstly a customer may use the financial institution purely as a repository of cash. This type of customer will be seeking a good return on savings and an efficient money transmission service. By this I mean that standing orders, direct debits and the like will be set up and executed correctly, that automatic telling machines will be stocked with cash and working, and that credits and debits are applied correctly and quickly. You would need to have been living on Mars for the last five years to have missed the efforts all the financial institutions have made to improve in this area. You should similarly be aware that the new entrants into the financial services industry (e.g. supermarkets, postal banks and major retailers) have centred much of their marketing effort on service and on the superior levels of interest rate paid. These customers are creditors of the financial institution. Without them retail financial institutions would not survive. Indeed many mutual financial institutions (building societies to you and me) have sought, and achieved, bank status to reduce their reliance on such customers.

Some customers are pure borrowers. This is very rare. Their main motivation is cost effectiveness. This is normally seen in the interest and charges applied to the borrowed monies. These customers are debtors of the financial institution.

Most customers are both creditors and debtors. That is they have accounts that operate in credit, and accounts that are always in deficit[1].

If service and high interest rates paid on deposits motivate people to open credit accounts, do service and low interest rates prompt people to become borrowers?

In general terms no. Most customers only borrow to meet one of two financial needs. The first of these is to overcome liquidity problems and the second is for asset purchase of one description or another. One might even argue that the old investment driving forces of *fear*

[1] Obviously such an account will have a repayment profile.

and greed are applicable to borrowers. Consider for a moment the customer who sees a pair of shoes in a sale. It is a week before payday and he or she does not really need a new pair of shoes, nor can they really be afforded until payday. This could be defined as a cash-flow problem. There are two solutions. One – do not buy the shoes: no expenditure – no need for borrowing. Solution two – give into the greed and buy the shoes with borrowed funds. In this case the loan will be repaid in a few days. Obviously the more expensive the asset purchased the longer the debt will need to be. The motivation here is greed.

The customer may face a number of unpleasant outcomes because of cash-flow problems (eviction, hunger, repossession of assets, etc). Is it too outrageous to suggest that the fear of these outcomes will drive a customer to seek short-term borrowing facilities from a financial institution? This is not to say that every potential borrower is so fearful of unpleasant outcomes or so greedy that he or she will be constructing a proposal that is untruthful. Indeed very few such proposals will be seen. Most, in fact, will be honestly made. However the prudent lender will be sensitive to the driving forces behind a request and take them into account.

Before we leave this area you might want to consider the amount of advertising the financial services industry does to promote the various borrowing facilities available. Would you agree that the major thrust is pandering to the greed of potential customers? While on the subject, what driving force are insurance companies trying to stimulate? Your later studies in marketing will take you further into this fascinating area.

Having looked at customer motivations let us begin to look at the range of customers. These are as follows:

Personal[2]

i)   individuals;

ii) joint;

iii) miscellaneous:

    a) clubs/associations;

    b) trustees and executors.

Business

i)   sole traders;

ii) partners;

iii) limited companies;

iv) public limited companies.

Personal

Individual

The first account most people open is their individual account. Normally on going to university

---

[2] A private individual who maintains an account (including a joint account with another private individual or an account held as an executor or trustee, but excluding the accounts of sole trader, clubs or societies) or who takes other services from a bank or building society.

or starting a job individuals find that they require a number of services that financial institutions specialize in. These are primarily the receipt and collection of monies from third parties and the ability to make payments from those funds. Given that most of the funds paid into an account will not be in the form of notes and coins but of cheques or electronic payments we can deduce what the primary concern of a financial institution must be. Put simply we must formally and accurately establish the identity of the potential customer from whom we will accept monies. The best and most reliable means of doing this is to obtain some form of official document that positively proves that Christopher Thomas Parry is who he says he is. This document should incorporate a signature (a passport or driving licence would be suitable) and perhaps a photograph. Of the two the signature is by far the most important, because it is against the signature that payments will be made by the financial institution. It would not be too grand a claim to say that the basis of modern financial services is that instructions to pay money out are made not in person but in writing. It is therefore essential that the signature be known with certainty. We will also be keen to establish an address for the potential customer and details of his or her current financial circumstances. This can be achieved by undertaking a credit reference search with an established credit reference agency. There are two main such agencies in the UK:

Experian Ltd.[3] and Equifax Europe Ltd.[4]

Presuming these investigations are satisfactory, the financial institution will open the account after completing an appropriate mandate. This is a standard document that sets out the operating instructions of the account. In most cases the account of an individual is classed as a *personal account*. However, there will be many instances when the individual is a *sole trader* and the ramifications of this will be considered later in the chapter.

Joint account

Far more likely than being a sole trader is that at some point after opening the first account our personal customer will undergo a significant change. A partner will be found. This relationship will develop along reasonably well-known lines until the time arises when the joint account becomes a necessity.

With a joint account the financial institution is dealing with two or more people on one account. The financial institution will probably know at least one of the parties who will be introducing the second, and may therefore choose to forgo the normal credit references – this may prove to be unwise for reasons that will become clear shortly. Although the normal checks and references may be waived, the financial institution will not forgo the completion of a *joint account mandate*.

This document will again set out the operating instructions of the account and specifically details of what combinations of signatures will serve as a valid authority for it to make payments from the joint account. In practice if it were anything other than "either to sign" this would place a heavy burden on the financial institution to physically inspect every cheque drawn on the account to ensure that the cheque was signed by both parties. You will be only

[3] PO Box 8000 Nottingham NG1 5GX 0115 9581111.
[4] Dept. 1E PO Box 3001, Glasgow G81 2DT 0990 7837873.

too aware of how labour-intensive this would be. A problem would arise if payment were made on a cheque signed by only one of the parties because there then could be a liability to the other partner should the second party dispute the payment (*Catlin v. Cyprus Finance Corporation (London) Limited*).

It is, however, just conceivable that the financial institution will accept a joint account on a "both to sign" basis. What it will not waive is the mandate condition that establishes the *joint and several liability* of both parties on the account.

This principle means that in the event of a debt on the account the parties will be both jointly liable for the debt *and individually* liable. This liability is regardless of who signed any (and all) cheques that caused the indebtedness. Under the principle of joint and several liability the financial institution can then seek redress on three fronts. Take the following, reasonably common, scenario:

Mr and Mrs Smith owe Haliwest Bank plc on a joint personal loan. No repayments have been made for six months and it appears that Mr Smith has disappeared. In order to reclaim the money the bank can sue:

1) Mr Smith

2) Mrs Smith

3) Mr and Mrs Smith

The first stage in the process of being repaid would be to set off any credit funds on either (or both) of the individual accounts against the joint debt[5].

Set-off
Involves applying credit balances on account A against debit balances on account B.

Example One

Mr Smith	Current Account Balance	250 Dr.
Mrs Smith	Current Account Balance	6,500 Cr.
Mr and Mrs Smith	Joint Personal Loan	5,000 Dr.

The bank can set off the 6500 Cr. against the 5000 Dr. repaying the loan in its entirety. Mrs Smith would be left with 1500.

Example Two

Mr Smith	Current Account Balance	250 Dr.
Mrs Smith	Current Account Balance	6,500 Cr.
Mr and Mrs Smith	Joint Personal Loan	15,000 Dr.

---

[5] There is no reverse right of set-off unless specifically agreed between the parties.

In this case there would be a net debt of £8,500. In this scenario the bank could issue actions against all three simultaneously but to save costs the claim would first be made against the defendant most likely to be able to pay.

If the first action proves unsuccessful or only partly successful then the bank can continue to proceed against the other parties until the debt is discharged or all avenues have been exhausted.

An important factor to bear in mind with joint accounts that are borrowing is that notice of dispute between the parties cancels the mandate – thus cancelling the bank's authority to make payments and making it open to claims under *Catlin*.

You will notice from the two preceding examples that the existence of a joint account does not exclude the existence of one or more sole accounts. Indeed it is possible that Mr Smith might have a number one account and a number two account. Here a right of set-off would still apply. In addition to the sole account and the joint account with his wife, Mr Smith may also be a sole trader and have one or more accounts in relation to that.

Minors

Another special type of individual account is that of *minors* which can be defined as:

Anyone under the age of 18[6]

We said earlier that a personal account was often first opened when going to university or starting a job. This is true. In a large number of cases, however, accounts will be opened for those under eighteen. These accounts are primarily used as a home for birthday/Christmas money and can over the years build into a substantial amount.

Should any special considerations be given prior to opening this type of account?

Generally it will be simple enough to prove the identity of the child because his or her parent(s) – or guardians – will be existing customers and act as introducer, and additionally we will be confident of the address. The first problem occurs with regards to the signature. Obviously a two-year-old has no discernable signature but does a seven-year-old? Or a sixteen-year old?

Research time – go and find out.

The main point of concern (in business terms) in relation to minors is the fact that they do not possess *the capacity to contract*. That is, they do not have the power to enter into legally binding contracts including contracts to borrow money. In the normal course of business the majority of minors will utilize the money holding and money transmission services of their financial institution. There may, however, on occasion be a request from a minor to borrow. Although the minor may be a customer of long standing, the lack of contractual capacity means that any debt incurred is not enforceable under normal circumstances[7]. The lender

---

[6] Family Law Reform Act 1969.
[7] For banking purposes these are limited to lending for necessities.

asked to supply funds to a twelve-year-old for the purchase of a Play Station®[8] would be hard pressed to prove the necessity of the same (regardless of what my son thinks!).

Where a lender does enter into a debt relationship with a minor the danger is that the repayment programme agreed may fall into default due not to an inability to repay, but rather to an unwillingness to repay. In such a circumstance the bank has three options open to it:

1. Write off the debt.

2. Seek redress under the Minor Contracts Act 1987.

3. Wait until the debtor attains maturity and trust (*hope?*) that the borrower will ratify the debt.

For all sorts of reasons – not least the bad publicity inherent in suing children – Option 1 is used most often.

Given, however, that prevention is better than cure, it is probably best to avoid lending to minors unless a guarantee[9] has been taken. In most cases the practical solution would be to lend the money to the parent/guardian, subject, of course, to normal lending criteria.

Despite the minor problem of lending to minors (pun intended) you will, of course, beware of how actively your financial institution promotes accounts for minors and seeks to open as many as possible through schools, banks and gifts. The reason for this is that children grow up and become adults (with contractual capacity) who can be lent to profitably. *Catch them young* seems to be the watchword. This process is even more pronounced with the accounts of university students. Certainly all the major banks offer interest-free overdrafts, cheap credit cards and loans to students in the hope of keeping their custom (and thus profit) for life.

Before we leave our consideration of personal accounts we should also consider other accounts opened by individuals and groups of individuals.

Sole traders

A sole trader is a person who is running a business as its sole owner. In many cases he or she work alone and employ no staff. However he or she may employ people – three or three hundred. If he is a one-man band the mandate will be reasonably simple. If, however, he or she is an employer, it may well be necessary for the mandate to reflect the fact that one or more employees will have the right to sign cheques, etc. on the trader's behalf. Does this mean that such an employee partakes in the liability for any debts incurred? *No.* The ability to sign on behalf of the employee does not imply joint liability. The employee is different from the business. In some cases the sole trader himself makes a distinction between his business and personal affairs. This is, however, incorrect. As far as English law is concerned the business is indistinguishable from the individual even though many sole traders will differentiate between their business and personal affairs by adopting a business or trading name. For example Joe Bloggs may run a business trading as Bloggs Car Services. In practice there will be two accounts opened:

[8] A trade mark registered by The Sony Corporation.
[9] A promise to repay by a third party.

Joe Bloggs Personal Account

Joe Bloggs trading as "Bloggs Car Services" Business Account

As far as the law[10] is concerned, any money lent to Bloggs Car Services is in fact lent to Joe Bloggs and Joe cannot avoid the debt on the grounds that the debt was incurred by the business. In practical terms the only difference between the two accounts is in the area of account charges. Most financial institutions levy limited charges on personal accounts and only then when the account is using borrowing facilities. With regard to the accounts of a sole trader the financial institution charges either a quarterly fee or a turnover fee to reflect the extra work and expertise involved in providing services to business customers.

Trustee/Executors/Administrators

Trustee

A person, or persons, appointed by a trust deed, to administer the affairs of another.

A trustee may be appointed to control assets until a minor reaches legal maturity. He or she may be appointed under the terms of a will to continue to run the affairs of the testator,[11] or may be appointed to act on behalf of a non-incorporated body such as a charity, club or association.

The trust deed is the document of primary importance here, and must be seen before an account is opened and carefully scrutinized to discover what, if any, borrowing is permitted and to discover any limitations to the borrowing capacity. It is important to note that where the trust deed has appointed more than one trustee (as is often the case), the account must be operated by both or all must sign mandates. If borrowing facilities are extended to the trustees, care should be taken to establish joint and several liability of all the trustees, so that in the event of default the lender has several possible courses of action.

You should be aware that unless the trust deed *specifically* gives the power to borrow then the power does not exist.[12].

Lending may be made available to a trustee who was seeking to sell the business of a deceased person. It makes sense that the business is sold as a *going concern* because this will generate greatest benefit for the beneficiaries. There could, perhaps, be a problem if the beneficiaries believed that the trustee had continued trading for too long (assisted by bank lending), thus losing them money.

Executor

A person, or persons, appointed under a will to wind up the affairs of the deceased.

An executor is appointed under the terms of a will to wind up the affairs of the deceased and may well require borrowing facilities to complete the task. This often involves a loan to pay inheritance tax to the Inland Revenue. In this circumstance the lender will need to see the following items:

[10] and the financial institution.
[11] Person making the will.
[12] There *may* be occasions when the Trustee Act 1925 will permit borrowing.

1. The will that appoints the executor.

2. The grant of probate given the court, confirming the executor.

3. The financial statement of the assets and liabilities of the deceased. This should evidence the level of inheritance tax payable and, importantly, the source of repayment. It might be that assets will need to be sold to repay the lending and this might, depending on the assets, take some time.

This type of lending is quite common and the executor(s) are personally liable. So again, joint and several guarantees should be taken.

Administrator

> A person, or persons, legally authorized by a court to administer the estate and/or affairs of another.

The commonest situations in which a personal administrator is appointed are:

1. A person dies without having made a will (intestate).

   Here the same considerations as for executors would apply, although letters of administration will be given by the court because there is no will to probate.

2) A person is adjudged by doctors and the court to be incapable of handling his or her own affairs.

In the normal course of events, the first the financial institution knows of the mental incapacity of their customer is when the receiver appointed by the court contacts it. The account of the patient is stopped and a new account opened in the name of the receiver.

It would be extremely rare for borrowing to be entertained in these circumstances, because most of the spending for a person in this situation should be for necessities. On the very rare occasions where lending is granted, the guarantee of the receiver should be taken.

Clubs and associations

These are groupings of people who share a common aim or purpose. This might be related to a common sporting interest or other pastime. In these circumstances the group usually formalizes the arrangement by forming a club. This formalization is often evidenced by the collection of annual subscriptions, the appointment of officers and the opening of a club, or association, bank account. This can present a few problems to the financial institution. In practice when the club is formed the first treasurer often opens the account with his or her own bankers and so the identity of at least one of the officers is established. However, the club mandate normally requires more than one officer to sign instructions to the bank. Does the bank take references on the other officers? If it is prudent, yes. The first problem arises when, as regularly happens, the original officers leave the club or relinquish office and their replacements, in all probability, are not known to you. Your immediate action is to amend the mandate to reflect the new signatories on the account but the question arises – do you know any of the new officers? If not, do you need to prove their identity? Some financial institutions do not bother, relying on the implied introduction of the outgoing officers, whereas others make basic account-opening enquiries.

Research time again – what does your organization do?

The major difficulty with the accounts of clubs and associations occurs on the rare occasions that a borrowing request is received. This difficulty arises from the fact that a club has no distinct and separate legal identity and consequently no capacity to enter into a contract to borrow. Consider the scenario in which you have lent £500 to the AllSwim Diving Club to purchase some group diving gear. The decision was made because the request was received from the treasurer Mr W.E. Know who, in addition to his personal and joint accounts held with you, is also the Managing Director of your largest corporate customer to whom you are lending £1,000,000. He is very highly regarded. The debt is being repaid as planned by standing order until one day your client requests a change of mandate form as he has left AllSwim Diving Club and joined AllDive Swimming Club. The new treasurer, he informs you, is a Mr S.T. Ranger who, he believes, has accounts with a competitor bank. In due course Mr Ranger calls to see you and says that "the club will be maintaining the account with you but could you explain the debt of £500?"

Against whom would you be able to enforce the debt?

AllSwim has no legal identity and capacity to enter into borrowing.

Mr W.E. Know points out that the loan was in the club's name and he is no longer in the club and while he knows no reason why the club should not continue to repay the loan there is nothing he can do to help you.

Mr Ranger maintains that the debt is not the club's and that the club has no record of having received the group diving gear and, most importantly, the club has no capacity to enter into a loan.

You do not know the other members of the club. (And it would do you no good if you did!)

In this situation you are likely to be left with egg on your face and a debt to be written off. From your accountancy studies you will recall that a debt written off reduces profits – this is not a good thing.

There are four ways to avoid this situation:

1. Do not lend to clubs.

2. Restrict lending to asset purchase and lend to the trustees of the club who will be the legal owners of the asset. Generally joint and several guarantees of the trustees will support the lending. We shall look at the problems associated with all types of guarantees in Chapter 8.

3. Lend for the group diving gear but take Mr W.E. Know's guarantee.

4. Do not lend to clubs.

Bankruptcy

Before considering non-personal oriented accounts we need to consider the situation of *bankruptcy*. A bankrupt is a person who has been deemed by the court as being unable to repay his or her debts. The person owed the money, or creditor[13], can apply (petition) for a bankruptcy order. In addition a person who has committed a crime and been tried in Crown Court can, if found guilty, be made criminally bankrupt. As a consequence of the bankruptcy order a trustee in bankruptcy will be appointed to realize and distribute the debtor's assets to repay the creditors. In effect this trustee takes over the financial affairs of the bankrupt and all such dealings should be via the trustee.

The undischarged bankrupt has a number of restrictions that will affect the financial institution. These are primarily the prohibition from:

1. Acting as a company director.

2. Engaging in business.

3. Holding public office, e.g. Member of Parliament.

4. Obtaining credit or borrow money.

How do we deal with these restrictions?

With a sole account the account must be stopped and all dealings must be with the trustee. Note that the bankruptcy order means all accounts are stopped. The personal account of Joe Bloggs and Joe Bloggs trading as Bloggs Car Services are both covered because legally there is no difference between the individual and his existence as a sole trader. With a joint account the account is again stopped but the joint instructions of the trustee and non-bankrupt customer should be followed.

A claim for any unsecured borrowing in the name of the customer must be made to the trustee who will, after realizing the assets, make a payment – normally x pence in the pound[14] – to all the unsecured creditors. If the customer had given security for the borrowing this must be realized. Any surplus is paid to the trustee and any shortfall is claimed on an unsecured basis.

Normally dealing with the accounts of a bankrupt is reasonably straightforward and each organization will have a well-defined process laid down on how to proceed. The main problem is where an account for an undischarged bankrupt is opened in error. Remember the undischarged bankrupt has lost control of financial affairs, which have passed to the trustee. The trustee is obviously interested in monies received after the bankruptcy because these may be due to the creditors. Indeed the trustee has the power to claim *after-acquired property* for up to 42 days. This would mean that any and all monies paid in must be held in the account for 42 days and permission sought from the trustee before payment is made. Obviously this is practically impossible and the only sensible course of action is not to open accounts for

[13] This includes a financial institution owed more than £750 on an unsecured basis.
[14] x will be less than 100.

undischarged bankrupts.

The world being what it is there have been several occasions when accounts have been opened for undischarged bankrupts who have not declared their status or who have used assumed names. If this occurs[15] then, if the situation were ever discovered, the financial institution might, in some circumstances, be liable for having paid away after-acquired property. In such a case the financial institution would have to compensate the trustee on behalf of the creditors. Once the deception is discovered the account must be stopped and the trustee in bankruptcy contacted. The trustee may declare that he or she has no interest in the account and the financial institution *could,* if it wanted, continue to operate the account. However, given that trust and honesty is the most important element of the banker/relationship, it is most likely that the account would be closed.

Generally a bankrupt (other than a criminal bankrupt) is automatically discharged after three years and regains full contractual capacity. This means he or she can open bank accounts and again borrow money. The rule of law in England and Wales is such that, once "time has been served", the offence is gone and should no longer be considered. Should a lender ignore the fact of a bankruptcy when considering a loan request? Or should the fact that a person was at one point made bankrupt mean that he or she will never be able to borrow again? We shall return to this question in Chapter 4 but:

Research time again – ask around, read internal regulations.

We shall consider the implications of bankruptcy of partners and company directors later in the chapter.

Business

Partnerships

Earlier in the chapter we painted the scenario of our basic, individual borrower finding a partner and opening a joint account. Obviously this may be romantic or because of other social reasons, but often the partnership will be:

To carry on a business in common with a view of profit[16]

Since 1890 a business partnership is deemed to exist if the definition can be applied to the business. Under the terms of the Act (which is still the defining legislation over 100 years later) partnerships are defined as being either as:

Trading or Non-trading Partnerships

Trading partnerships are limited in numbers to 20 partners and can be groupings of skilled tradesmen such as painters, mechanics, etc.

Non-trading partnerships, in contrast, which include, for example, accountants, solicitors and dentists (this is not an exhaustive list), are not restricted to a maximum of 20 partners.

[15] This is another reason for establishing identity at the outset.
[16] Section (1) Partnership Act 1890.

Normally the partnership will consist of general partners. Each partner will take an active part in the business and management of the business. Each general partner will have contributed funds into the business and will be entitled to a proportion of the profits. Importantly he or she will, jointly with other partners, be liable for the debts of the partnership.

Occasionally the partnerships may contain:

- *Limited Partners*: These, as the name suggests, have only limited liability for the debts of the partnership. This amount is the amount of the capital injected. They will also have a limited share of the profits.

- *Sleeping Partners*: This type of partner receives a share of the profits but takes no part in the day-to-day business or management of the business. They are also fully liable for debts.

- *Salaried Partners*: This type of partner receives a salary in lieu of profit share but is not liable for the debts of the partnership.

A full study of the rights, duties and obligations of these types of partners is beyond the scope of this course but will be looked at in other modules. In your studies, you may assume that all partners are general partners.

The Partnership Act also gives the power to the partnership to:

1) *own assets*

   Both types of partnerships are permitted to own assets. An asset is considered to be owned jointly by the partners provided it is bought with partnership money or brought into the partnership when the partnership was formed. The use of a property owned by a partner does not make that property partnership property.

2) *borrow*

   Trading partnerships have implied powers to borrow and pledge security.

   Non-trading partnerships do not have an implied authority to borrow, although the partners can take this power either via a partnership agreement or through the bank account mandate.

   Obviously if the partnership is borrowing and defaults, the question arises, "Who is responsible for the debt"? The key to the answer lies in whether a partnership is a separate legal entity distinct from the partners. The answer is a resounding *no!* Liability for the borrowing, therefore, rests with the partners *jointly*. Financial institutions have, however, long utilized mandates that expand this joint liability to *joint and several liability*. As with joint accounts, this means that each partner is fully responsible for all the partnership debts. We should, as lenders, therefore be sure of the identity of all the partners and the practise of credit references, etc. is indispensable.

3) *permitted to trade under a name other than that of the partners*

   For example Bloggs and his new partner Mr J.Ames may decide to continue to trade under the name Bloggs Car Services (and benefit from the reputation of the business) rather than trade as Bloggs and Ames. In this case the account, and any subsequent borrowing, will be in the name of Bloggs Car Services.

Obviously the mandate used when opening the account of a partnership is of vital importance. As already mentioned the mandate will create joint and several liability and will specify the signing instructions. Unlike the joint account of Mr and Mrs Smith, which will have an either-to-sign mandate, the mandate of a business partnership may contain several levels of authority. For example cheques[17] of up to, say, £150 may be signed by any of the partners. Cheques in the range £151 to £250 by any two, and cheques over £250 by all partners.

Back to bankruptcies. Obviously if one of the partners becomes bankrupt that partner loses the right to engage in business. The partnership account must, therefore, be stopped immediately. Some partnership agreements acknowledge that bankruptcy might happen and allow for it. Normally the bankrupt partner sells his or her share of the partnership to a third party or the remaining partners. The proceeds are obviously paid to the trustee in bankruptcy. If a partnership agreement does not exist or does not cover this aspect, the partnership is automatically dissolved even if the remaining partners are not bankrupt. In all likelihood the remaining, non-bankrupt, partners will open a new account in the name of a new partnership.

It is of course possible that the partnership itself could become insolvent. This may or may not mean the bankruptcy of all the partners and great care would be needed to ascertain the actual type of insolvency. If the order were made under the Insolvent Partnerships Order 1994 then the insolvency would apply only to the partnership and not to the individual partners and so only the partnership account would be stopped. Otherwise the partnership account and the personal (and joint) accounts of any partner also held by you must be stopped.

Limited company

As an alternative to forming a partnership Bloggs and Ames may decide to form a *limited company*. There are advantages and disadvantages to this course of action and you should be familiar with some of these from your studies in Accountancy. The most important advantage of forming a limited company is the concept of limited liability. This important advantage derives from the following landmark legal ruling from 1897:

> *A limited company is a separate legal entity from its owners.*
>
> *Salomon v. Salomon and Co. Ltd.*

This means, essentially, that the company is not the directors, nor are the directors (or shareholders) the company. They are distinct and separate. Despite the amount of publicity and press coverage of big public limited companies (e.g. British Telecom plc, Marks and Spencer plc, National Westminster Bank plc, etc.), the majority of companies in the United Kingdom are *private limited companies*. There are several differences between them, but the *corporate veil* covers both of them.

---

[17] Or any written instructions.

Private limited companies: commonly abbreviated to Ltd.

Generally small organizations with little share capital. A private limited company may have a large number of shareholders but needs only one. This shareholder would be the director (but cannot also be the secretary) and exercise total control over the running of the company. Most of the private limited companies holding accounts with you will have between two and five directors, who will also own the share capital. As you already know, the more shares you own the greater the degree of control you have.

Public limited companies: commonly abbreviated to plc.

Generally much larger both in terms of share capital and number of directors (minimum two) and overall shareholder numbers. Most of the plcs that we hear about on a daily basis are household names, employing large numbers of people and making large profits. However you would not progress much further in you studies thinking that every public limited company shares these characteristics. Although the largest company (in terms of market capitalization[18]) is valued at almost £80,000,000,000, the two-hundredth is valued at only about £700,000,000.

> *Research Time again – How many companies are listed on the London Stock Exchange and what is the average market capitalization?[19]. Most plcs are far, far smaller in terms of capitalization, employees and profits. The suffix plc does not guarantee success, either for the business or the lender.*

Alternative Investment Market (AIM)

You may also be aware that some limited companies grow and expand. Often the best way forward for them is to become plcs. Most do this initially via the Alternative Investment Market (AIM)

As the name suggests the plc can sell its shares to members of the public (which a private limited company is barred from doing). A *board of directors* runs the plc and the members of the board (who are probably shareholders) are appointed by the shareholders at *annual general meetings*. The *directors* are responsible for the overall strategy and direction of the company and, in most cases, the day-to-day matters may be in the hands of the *chief executive* and other employed managers. You should be aware that in our largest plcs, institutional investors and not individuals hold the majority of the share capital. These *institutional investors* (the term *fund manager* is also used here) often own sufficient shares to be a board member by right and he or she will represent the interest of the institutional investor. It is highly unlikely that the chief executive of a major plc is also be the majority shareholder, although many CEOs have large shareholdings.

> *Research time – How many shares does your chief executive own?*

Before moving on, the following quotation may help to bring the role of institutional investors into focus.

[18] Share price multiplied by number of shares.
[19] Clue: go and buy a *Financial Times* and try the inside back cover.

Peter Butler, a director of Hermes, one of Britain's most powerful fund managers, picked up the phone last Monday (26 January 1999) and dialled Sir Victor Blank, chairman of the embattled Mirror Group. His agenda was simple: he said David Montgomery, the newspaper group's chief executive, was a disaster and he wanted him removed from the board. Hermes … was one of several Mirror Group investors agitating for change.

John Waples, *Sunday Times*, 31 January 1999

Mr Waples goes on to say:

In recent weeks the City has seen a series of high-profile takeovers, mergers and board room sackings initiated as a result of intervention by a handful of the country's biggest institutions.

His article concludes:

To date, fund managers have shown themselves quite good at sacking chief executives but that is usually the easy bit. Recruiting new managers capable of producing growth strategies in a low inflation world is a lot harder.

As far as the examination is concerned you can safely assume that all the companies you will be asked to consider will be small- to medium-sized private limited companies. At this stage you will not be expected to consider the complexities of a plc.

Legal position

Following the *Saloman v. Saloman & Co. Ltd.* case, the principle of limited liability and corporate entity became established. Like that other legal entity – a person – a company can own assets (including property). It can hire staff and be hired. It can sue and be sued. On the differences side, unlike humans the company does not have a finite lifetime[20]. It does not cease to exist if a shareholder, or shareholders, die. Nor does it cease to exist if shareholders transfer their shares to others. Each shareholder knows the full extent of liability for company debts. Normally this will be zero, although if a shareholder has *partly-paid* shares then there will be a liability equal to the amount unpaid on the shares – and no more. Unlike most partnerships, it is not restricted in the number of shareholders it can have. On the downside, it must submit its accounts to Companies House on an annual basis and these are available for scrutiny by both the public and its competitors. This is something that neither sole traders nor partnerships have to do.

The key outcome of *Saloman* is that the owners (shareholders) of a company are not liable for the debts of the company provided their shares have been fully paid.[21]

While partnerships are still governed by the 1890 Act, the law has moved on in terms of companies and the primary legislation governing the actions of companies are the Companies Act 1985 and the Companies Act 1989.

The practical implications from the point of view of the financial institution are as follows:

[20] Unless it fails financially – liquidation – more of this later.
[21] If partly paid the liability is limited to the amount unpaid on the shares not the totality of the company's debts.

1) The account will be opened in the name of the limited company. The difficulty is that we obviously have no driving licence or passport to prove the identity of the potential customer. What is available is the *certificate of incorporation* and, for public limited companies, the *trading certificate*. Each of these documents incorporates the company's name (rather like a birth certificate) and while there are some restrictions (not to be offensive or too similar to another pre-existing name), a company can call itself almost anything. It is not, however, obliged to trade under the registered name and could choose the legend Bloggs and Ames Ltd. Trading as Bloggs Car Services

   To trade as Bloggs Car Services the company must disclose the true status of the business on all its stationery and at the place of business.

2) Although the company has a "birth certificate" – and even at this young age has the capacity to contract – it does not have obvious means of interacting with the outside world. This is the role of the directors. Directors are appointed by the shareholders (and will most likely be shareholders) to run the affairs of the company on a day-to-day basis. It is the directors who will sign cheques and standing orders. It is the directors who will deal with suppliers and customers and the directors who will negotiate with financial institutions for banking and borrowing facilities. Should we therefore conduct credit reference and other enquiries on the directors? *No.* The directors are not the company and the company is not the directors – they are distinct legal entities. The only concern we need to have with regards to directors is – are they undischarged bankrupts? You will remember from earlier that an undischarged bankrupt cannot run a business. This means that they cannot take part in running a company. If after opening the account for X Ltd., one of the directors becomes bankrupt then the only action required is to amend the mandate to remove the signing authority of said bankrupt. The bankruptcy does not automatically remove them as shareholders, although the voting rights of the shares will pass to the trustee in bankruptcy who may in due course sell them.

The directors, as representatives of the shareholders, must follow the rules of the company. These rules are enshrined in the *memorandum of association* and the *articles of association* and these, respectively, regulate the external and internal dealings of the company. What exactly do these memorandum and articles of association contain?

Memorandum of association

a) The *name* of the company – including Ltd. or plc.

b) The *registered office* – this is the address where the company is deemed to "live". It is to this address that writs can be served on the company. A company can trade from any number of addresses but it can have only one registered office. Consider how many branches your organization has. The registered office also determines the legal system to which the company is subject. For example, a company with a registered office in London, Manchester, Birmingham or Cardiff is subject to English law whereas companies whose registered office is Glasgow or Edinburgh are subject to Scottish law.[22]

[22] If I was being paid by the word just think how much fun I could have had in this sentence!

As far as the examination is concerned you will be concerned only with English law which, as you should know, covers Wales.

c) The *objectives clause* – this states what the company is allowed to do. Most companies will, in addition to listing their main objectives, have a catch-all clause along the lines of "and anything else we can think of".[23]

d) *Statement of shareholder liability.*

e) The *association clause* – details of the original shareholders. It is not that difficult to start a limited company. In fact one can be bought off-the-shelf. The original shareholders would be perhaps a solicitor or an accountant.

Articles of association

In general terms these govern:

a) Powers and duties of directors.

b) Issue and transfer of shares.

c) Rights of shareholders.

d) Appointment (and removal) of directors.

e) Conduct of the meetings of the company[24].

The Companies Act 1985 contains a model articles of association (Table A) that companies can adopt and, if necessary, amend to suit individual circumstances. Most companies in fact do this.

Once drafted, the articles are approved by the original shareholders and registered with the Registrar of Companies.

Perhaps the most important aspect to concern ourselves with, in this course, is the role of the directors. This is crucial – it is the directors who will negotiate borrowings on behalf of the company and pledge the assets of the company (if required) as security. When I entered banking this caused some problems, because a lender needed to ensure that the company (and the directors) had the power to borrow and pledge security, and there were several cases when they did not! In those cases the borrowing and the security would be voided. Since the Companies Act 1989 this has, happily, changed because Section 35B states:

> *A party to a transaction with a company is not bound to enquire as to whether it[25] is permitted by the company's memorandum or as to any limitation on the powers of the board of directors to bind the company or authorize others to do so.*

Under this section a debt can no longer be avoided because the company and/or its directors acted outside its powers (*ultra vires*) as expressed in its memorandum and articles of association. The lender is protected provided that the purpose of the loan was commercially justified.

---

[23] My own paraphrasing.
[24] The annual general meeting is the most important but there are also general and special meetings.
[25] The transaction.

Company funding

Before we leave companies we should spend a little time considering how companies are funded. With a sole trader the entire assets of the individual back the business enterprise. With a partnership each partner injects some capital to start the enterprise while remaining liable for the debts of the business. What about a company?

A company issues shares. These are generally called *ordinary shares* and are the predominant element of a company's capital. A shareholder effectively gives money to the company to use as it sees fit. The company is under no obligation to repay the shareholder although it will be expected to pay the shareholder a share of the profits earned. This payment is called a *dividend* and may be paid annually or bi-annually. The dividend is not guaranteed. With a private limited company there may well be restrictions on the transfer of the shares but in a plc the shares have no restrictions on transferability.

Although the ordinary shares will always be the mainstay within the capital structure of every company, there are three other methods a company can use to raise capital. These are:

1) preference shares;

2) loan stocks;

3) warrants.

Preference shares (Prefs)

Preference shares are, as the name suggests, preferred in some way. But in relation to whom and how? Simply put, the preference shareholders are preferred to the ordinary shareholders if the company is wound up, and in terms of dividends if profits are low.

A company may issue a limited number of, say, 7%[26] preference shares in addition to its ordinary shares. This means that when the company makes a profit, 7% (of the nominal value) must be paid to the preference shareholders before the ordinary shareholders get anything. The ordinary shareholder may get more or less than the preference shareholders. If the company does not declare a dividend neither type of shareholder gets anything. Many companies have also issued *cumulative prefs* – these have the added benefit of carrying forward any unpaid dividends to future years – again paid before the ordinaries get anything.

To finish off our study of prefs there are three more types:

1. *Participating* – In addition to their fixed percentage these shareholders get an additional payment after the dividend paid to the ordinary shareholder rises above a certain level.

2. *Convertible* – Here the preference shares can be swapped for ordinary shares under certain conditions and at predetermined levels. For example:

    Four ordinary shares for eight preferences between June 2001 and December 2002.

3) *Redeemable* – Unlike ordinary shares some – very few – preference shares have a fixed repurchase date.

[26] Any percentage is possible.

It is possible to mix types and have 6% cumulative, redeemable, convertible preference shares – perm any name you want. You will not see them in the exam.

Loan Stocks

Again there are several types all sharing similar characteristics:

1. A fixed rate of interest payable regardless of whether or not a profit is made. Unlike dividends any interest paid is offset against tax.

2. A fixed repayment date.

These characteristics are shared by gilt-edged stock issued by the government and local authority bonds but are deemed more risky and the interest paid will generally be higher than gilts or LA bonds.

Company loan stocks can be secured (often called *debentures*[27]) or unsecured and in some cases can be converted into ordinary shares. Again this conversion would be under pre-agreed terms and conditions.

Many companies find loan stocks a useful source of funds. Generally finding them cheaper than bank loans and less contentious than share issues, most companies have some form of loan stock in the balance sheet. All loan stock will appear as long-term capital and holders of such stock are creditors of the company. The holders would get repaid before shareholders in liquidation.

Warrants

Warrants are the right, but not the obligation, to purchase shares at a fixed price on a fixed date in the future. For example, ABC plc is offering warrants for sale at 25p. Each warrant gives the holder the right to buy an ABC plc share in ten years at £1.50 per share. Currently ABC's shares are selling on the stock exchange for 70p.

The warrant buyer will make a profit if, in ten years, the share price of ABC plc has risen above £1.75 (£1.50 plus 25p). If the share price was £1, the right to buy at £1.50 would obviously not be exercised.

The funds the company receives from the warrants are part of the company's capital, but the company pays no dividends.

Liquidation

Many pages ago we said that a company does not have a finite life. This does not mean that it cannot die. Death for a company is called liquidation and is the corporate equivalent of bankruptcy. As with bankruptcy, a company can be wound up voluntarily by the members (shareholders) or by the creditors. In place of a trustee in bankruptcy a company will have a liquidator who will fulfil the same role. A *compulsory liquidation* ordered by the courts is also possible.

---

[27] In the UK debenture always signifies secured debt, but in the USA the term relates to unsecured debt.

Full details of the process of liquidation will be dealt with in other modules but it is appropriate to look at who gets what in liquidation.

1. *Creditors with security* – The asset given as security will be sold and any surplus paid to the liquidator. Any shortfall becomes an unsecured debt. Banks often take fixed charges over assets, especially if they lent the company the money to purchase the asset.

2. *Liquidator's expenses* – Well you don't expect an accountant to work for nothing do you?

3. *Preferential creditors:*

    - wages up to £800 per employee;

    - deductions collected from employees in respect of income tax or National Insurance;

    - Value Added Tax;

    - Social Security contributions;

    - any monies owing under pension scheme arrangements.

4. *Floating-charge holders* – We shall look at floating charges in more depth in Chapter 8. Banks often take floating charges.

5. *Unsecured creditors* – Generally suppliers.

6. *Shareholders* – If there is any money left at this stage – unlikely – the preferential shareholders get their funds back before the ordinary shareholders.

One final point on companies – unlike humans they cannot become mentally incapacitated.

Here endeth the second chapter. We have looked at the different types of customers that will generally be found in most branches. While there are major differences, there are some key points to remember:

1. Do we really know for certain that the customer is who he/she/it proports to be?

2. Who is authorized to issue instructions on behalf of the customer?

3. Who is authorized to borrow on behalf of the customer?

4. Who is responsible for repaying the borrowing if things go wrong?

3

LENDING FACILITIES

Can I have some leaflets on your loan facilities please?

Author, Jan. 99

Which ones? – We've got hundreds – but they are all the same really.

Bank Official, Jan. 99

What do you mean?

Author, Jan. 99

A loan is a loan is a loan. We just package them differently. They are all the same thing really.

Bank Official, Jan. 99

Just before commencing work on this chapter I visited a branch of a local clearing bank where the above conversation took place. Was the official correct? Is a loan just a loan?

The Pocket Oxford Dictionary[1] defines *loan* as:

Noun. – 1. Thing lent, esp. a sum of money. 2. Lending or being lent – verb – lend.

And in the Introduction we defined lending as:

1. *To grant the use of a thing on the understanding that it, or its equivalent, shall be returned.*

   or

2. *To allow the use of money at interest.*

Personally I think he was half right. Although permitting a customer the use of money is the same action, there are some radical differences that are more than merely packaging. However, at the end of this section, you may have come to agree with the official and disagree with me.

Earlier we looked at the reasons for borrowing which were summarized as:

[1] Oxford University Press. Eighth edition, 1996.

- short-term liquidity needs;

- asset purchase.

It will be useful to look at the facilities that meet these needs in the same order. Before doing that, however, let us list the major general loan facilities and their primary uses.

Facility	Primary Use
Overdrafts	Liquidity
Personal Loans	Asset Purchase
Ordinary Loans	Asset Purchase
Revolving Credit	Liquidity
Bridging Loans	Asset Purchase
Credit Cards	Liquidity
Probate Loans	Liquidity

3.1 Liquidity needs

There is a very old saying that nothing in life is certain except death and taxes. Almost as universal to the human experience (in Western society at least) is the cash-flow (or liquidity) problem. Remember Mr Micawber in Charles Dickens novel *David Copperfield*?

> *Annual income twenty pounds, annual expenditure nineteen pounds nineteen and sixpence, result happiness. Annual income twenty pounds, annual expenditure twenty pounds and sixpence, result misery.*

In the novel, Mr Micawber was always expecting something to turn up. In today's financial environment we do not need to wait for something to turn up because our liquid needs can be met from a wide variety of sources who are all, it seems, falling over themselves to lend us sufficient money to have today what we want today. If only dealing with the consequences of this availability were as simple.

Look below at the list of facilities available to meet liquidity needs.

- revolving credit;

- overdrafts;

- credit cards;

- probate loans.

The order is different from the previous list – not, as might be assumed, to make a simple mnemonic but to reflect the fact that all the various facilities that are geared towards meeting liquid needs are, at the bottom line, a form of revolving credit.

3.2   Revolving credit

Simply put, revolving credit involves the use of a pre-set credit (loan) limit operating in conjunction with a regular credit and debit based account. The term fluctuating balance account could also be used and would, in some senses, be more accurate.

For example if a revolving credit limit of £500 is set, the following transactions might occur.

Table 3.1

Limit	Payments made	Credits received	Balance	Available credit
500				500
	15		15 dr.	485
	25		40 dr.	460
	250		290 dr.	210
	150		440 dr.	60
		440	0	500

The essence is that, as the revolving credit facility is utilized, the amount of available credit reduces. As credits are received they reduce the amount of credit used and increase the credit available.

This scenario occurs in current accounts, charge cards and credit cards, although each displays unique features which we shall look at.

Current accounts

As you are well aware the current account is the main money transmission vehicle provided by banks and building societies to their customers. Primarily the customers have their salaries/wages paid into these accounts either electronically or by cash/cheque. Payments from these accounts are made in four different ways.

Direct debit

Whereby an organization (for example, a utilities company) collects from a customer's account an amount on a monthly (or other regular periodic) basis. The authority to do this is obviously the customer's written, signed instruction presented to the financial institution by the collecting company.

Standing order

Here the financial institution is instructed by the customer to make specific payments on specific dates to the payee.

Cheque

Written instructions of variable amounts presented through the clearing system by the payee.

Debit card

An electronic version of a cheque that uses electronic point-of-sale (EPOS) technology. A normal month may look something like this:

Table 3.2

Item	Type	Payment	Receipt	Balance
Salary	BACS		1500	1500
Mortgage	S/O	300		1200
Council tax	DD	75		1125
Water rates	DD	26		1099
House insurance	DD	35		1064
Car insurance	DD	24		1040
Life insurance	DD	89		951
Electricity	DD	45		906
Gas	DD	25		881
	EPOS	26.32		854.68
		12		842.68
		314		528.68
		110		418.68
		59		359.68
		46		313.68
	CHEQUE	212		101.68
		100		1.68

This would make Mr Micawber very happy. Next month might look like this:

Table 3.3

Item	Type	Payment	Receipt	Balance
Balance from previous month				1.68
Salary	BACS		1500	1501.68
Mortgage	S/O	300		1201.68
Council tax	DD	75		1126.68
Water rates	DD	26		1100.68
House insurance	DD	35		1065.68
Car insurance	DD	24		1041.68
Life insurance	DD	89		952.68
Electricity	DD	45		907.68
Gas	DD	25		882.68
	EPOS	35		847.68
		34		813.68
		114		699.68
		15		684.68
		59		625.68
		46		579.68
	CHEQUE	112		467.68
		80		387.68
		76		311.68
		32		279.68

No short-term liquidity needs here. Notice that, over the two months, the balance on the account has gone from 0 to 1500 to 1.68 to 1501.68 to 279.68 and could be said to be revolving.

Figure 3.1

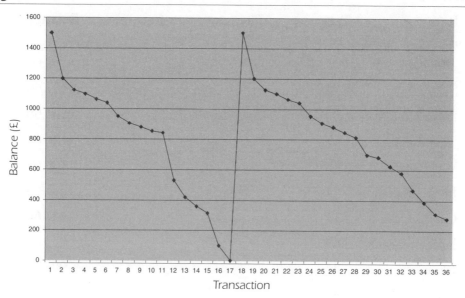

But consider the third month.

Table 3.4

Item	Type	Payment	Receipt	Balance
Balance from previous month	279.68			
Salary	BACS	1500	1779.68	
Mortgage	S/O	300	1479.68	
Council tax	DD	75	1404.68	
Water rates	DD	26	1378.68	
House insurance	DD	35	1343.68	
Car insurance	DD	24	1319.68	
Life insurance	DD	89	1230.68	
Electricity	DD	45	1185.68	
Gas	DD	25	1160.68	
	EPOS	650	510.68	
		48	462.68	

Item	Type	Payment	Receipt	Balance
		85	377.68	
		12	365.68	
		62	303.68	
		22	281.68	
	CHEQUE	99	182.68	
		74	108.68	
		89	19.68	
		59	-39.32	

Notice here that, before the regular salary has been received, the customer has a short-term liquidity need. He is overdrawn by £39.32. According to Mr Micawber – misery. And misery would certainly be the result if the financial institution did not obey the customer's written instruction (cheque) to pay out the £59. This misery would be caused to the reputation of the customer when the payee of the cheque discovered the non-payment. But what caused the overdraft? If we look at the payment profile the electronic point of sale debit of £650 has really caused the overdraft. Obviously at the time of making the large payment, the customer could afford it. It was only at the end of the month that the (perhaps unexpected) expense of £59 caused the problem.

Overdrafts
Salary Anticipation Limit (SAL)

This scenario leads to the most common of the overdrafts authorized by financial institutions – the *salary anticipation limit* (SAL). Most customers in receipt of a regular salary will, in the few days before salary receipt, need/want extra flexibility. One of the reasons for this is because most people get paid twelve times a year linked to calendar months which are not of even length. Obviously this does not effect the fixed regular payments – mortgage, rent, etc. but does affect such expenses as food, petrol, etc.

The financial institutions are left with a number of options:

• refuse to make payments that would put the account overdrawn;

• inspect every account that goes overdrawn and decide whether or not to wait for the salary to arrive.

The advantages of option one is that no unauthorized debts will be incurred and thus no unexpected bad debts created. The disadvantage is that no interest (and thus no profit) will be earned.

The second option has the advantage of opening the possibility of earning interest but is very time consuming.

To get round the disadvantages of each of the methods, and still retain the profit potential, most financial institutions will place a limit on the account of the customer without advising them. This limit will be linked to the expected salary and the perceived creditworthiness of the customer.

For example, a customer of six months standing and a regular salary of £1,000 per month might be given a salary anticipation limit (SAL) of £200. This means that, providing the account remains under £200 overdrawn, no bank official will spend time looking at the account but interest will still be earned.

A second customer, of perhaps three years standing, might have a SAL of £500 against the same expected salary.

In addition to this, normally unadvised, limit it is likely that customer will approach the financial institution for an approved overdraft limit at some point. This might be for a number of good reasons. For example:

- a family holiday;

- a large purchase;

- Christmas;

- emergency expenses.

In the majority of cases the financial institution will be keen to accommodate customers of long (good) standing. It enables them to establish the usefulness of the institution in the customer's mind and to build loyalty. Hopefully this loyalty will result in further business as the customer continues with the organization. One thing that is absolutely certain is that denying the request for an overdraft will result in the loss of the customer to a competitor. This is not to say for one moment that every request should be approved. Appropriate consideration should be given to every request. To summarize, the brief considerations are:

1) Is there already an unadvised salary limit in place?

   For a customer of long standing there may well be. If so the question to ask yourself is simple. "Does the existing SAL meet the requested need?" If it does, do not reinvent the wheel. Approve the overdraft for the customer.

2) How long does the customer want the facility for?

   - Any period longer than 12 months would be very uncomfortable. In practice a specific overdraft should be repaid within three months.

3) When and how will repayment be made?

   Acceptable hows? might be:

   - annual bonus payment from employer due:

     - question how certain – check records – what was it last year?

- proceeds from sale of asset:

    - question – value of asset/costs of selling;

        Selling an asset for £500 does not support an overdraft facility of £1,000. But vice versa is good.

- Benefit from a legacy:

    - check with solicitor re amount and date of expected receipt.

        (Expected legacies from not yet deceased relatives are not good sources for repayments of overdrafts)

- Transfer from a deposit account. Many customers will deposit most of their liquid resources in accounts paying higher rates of interest. This is often accompanied by a period of notice being required by the financial institution. If the money is deposited in-house you had better agree to the overdraft (provided there are sufficient funds to transfer). [2] If the funds are with a competitor them some evidence of deposit would be appropriate.[3]

Once the overdraft facility has been approved it is essential that care is taken to ensure that repayment actual happens. This will mean monitoring for receipt of the promised funds at the due time. For example, a regularly received request is for an overdraft to pay for the family holiday to be repaid on receipt of the regular annual bonus. The customer will be able to say that the payment is due in the August pay run.

In this case we would check the date of salary receipt and sanction the facility until then. In August a check would be made to ascertain if the funds have been received. This obviously applies also to the expected date of receipt of sale proceeds.

Care should also be taken to ensure that the position on the current account *after* bonus payment is in credit – or within the existing SAL. It is not unknown for people to spend more on holidays than expected – and more than the bonus. Within reason, this will not cause problems and customers will regularize the situation themselves within a few months. It may be appropriate to input a SAL at this point to keep the account off the exceptions report. Again it would be prudent to look at the account to see that the excess spend is being reduced. This would be seen by:

- the account returning to credit balances at the month end;

- the account showing reducing debit balances month by month.

You would become concerned if the account develops a *hard core* overdrawn position. This is displayed below.

---

[2] In this case you might want to consider offering a loan facility so that the customer can keep his or her deposit – subject to the customer being able to afford the loan repayments.

[3] Massive cross-selling opportunities here.

Figure 3.2: Hard-core position

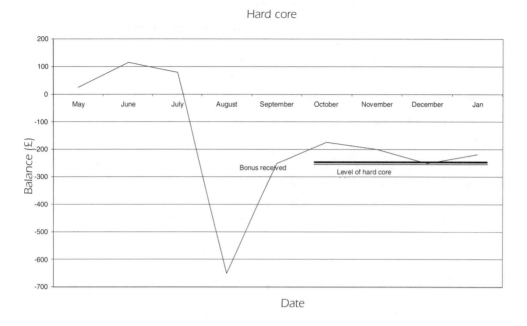

As we look at the graph we can see that the account went overdrawn, by agreement, and the expected bonus was received in August. Here the problems start.

Either the bonus was less than expected[4] or the holiday cost more than expected.

Notice how the account now never goes back into credit. The account has developed a debit that is not reducing. This is classic hard-core borrowing. This type of situation cannot be allowed to go investigated or ignored. In all probability the solution will be to capitalize the hard core on to a loan account with regular monthly repayments.

The advantage of this action is that eventually the debt is repaid and the customer stops paying interest on approximately £250 per month. Hard core can also develop within an account in an ordinary year and is often hidden by the SAL. It is always a good idea to look at the average balance on an account and the maximum and minimum balances for the last year before automatically renewing a SAL. Unspotted and/or ignored hard-core debit balances often end up as *bad or doubtful debts*.

Business Overdrafts

Overdraft facilities are not made available just to personal customers. Every type of business customer – indeed most businesses – will, at some point, request the use of an overdraft facility. Such requests raise a different group of questions arising from the nature of businesses. It is possible to classify businesses as:

● those that produce and sell their products;

4 Perhaps the customer forgot income tax and National Insurance. Call me a cynic but…

- e.g. farmers, car manufacturers;
- those that purchase pre-manufactured products and sell them on;
  - e.g. retail stores;
- Those that provide a service and receive payment for that service;
  - e.g. accountants/solicitors.

Very, very few businesses have elderly relatives leaving them money[5]. They do not benefit from bonus payments. They derive their income from the sales of their products or services. However, they do suffer from cash-flow problems. Take the farmer going to plant 400 acres of wheat (cost of seeds?) in spring to be sold in the autumn. He still has expenses while the wheat is growing and will likely need an overdraft to enable these expenses to be paid. Repayment would come from the sale of the wheat. Another example would be the Blackpool guesthouse owner. All summer long the guesthouse is full and funds are flowing in. However autumn comes and the number of guests falls. The fixed costs of the business do not. While most competent business people will budget for this and reserve excess summer income, it is possible that come April/May an overdraft facility will be needed.

The majority of well-run businesses will prepare *cash-flow forecasts*. We look at these in greater detail later, but a cash-flow forecast is a list of expected income less expenditure on a month-by-month (or week-by-week) for example:

Table 3.5

Month	1	2	3	4	5	6	7	8	9	10	11	12
Opening balance (thousands)	15	17	13	9	-1	-6	-16	-24	-15	-5	-3	-1
Monthly income	12	6	6	5	5	5	7	19	20	12	12	20
Monthly expenses	10	10	10	15	10	15	15	10	10	10	10	10
Net cash flow	2	-4	-4	-10	-5	-10	-8	9	10	2	2	10
Closing balance	17	13	9	-1	-6	-16	-24	-15	-5	-3	-1	9

You should notice the following points:

1. The closing balance in Month 1 is the sum of the opening balance of the month and the net cash flow.

2. The opening balance of Month 2 is the closing balance of month one.

3. Without an overdraft facility the business will be unable to trade from Month 4 onwards.

4. The position at the end of the year is back in credit – effectively the facility has been repaid. This repayment has come from sales income. A business can control its expenses

---

[5] Consideration of holding and parent companies is beyond the scope of this course.

(to a certain extent) but generating sales is harder. Falling sales income is a very worrying situation.

5.   The cash-flow forecast does not show that the business is profitable.

It is probable that the lender will mark a limit of £25,000 or even £30,000. This is because cash-flow forecasting is notoriously difficult and imprecise. A slight delay in receipt of cheques or an unanticipated increase in expenses will cause problems.

Most businesses will compare actual income and expenditure against the forecast and every lender should do the same by comparing the end-of-month balance against the projections. A balance of £16,500 at the end of Month 1 or £1,890 overdrawn in Month 4 would not be considered a cause for concern. However should the overdraft rise to £16,000 in Month 5 questions would need to be asked of the business. Yes £16,000 is within the facility approved but the level is well outside the projection. The business needs to explain why. Has a large expense expected in Month 6 actually been paid in Month 5? This would be an acceptable reason. What if the reason was no income in Month 6 and an unexpected £5,000 bill at the same time? Straightaway the lender knows that, even if the rest of the forecast is totally correct, the overdraft facility will be exceeded.

How then should a lender respond to this situation? The whole sanction needs to be re-evaluated. There is no point in waiting until Month 7 when the limit is breached.

To make a lender comfortable the management of the business should know what has happened and why. It must have a solution to the situation. The lender would be most comfortable with the management that advised them of the breakdown in the cash-flow forecast in Month 4 before the lender spotted it – even if this was accompanied by a revised cash flow and a request to increase the sanctioned limit.

The worst case scenario is were the management is unaware that its forecast has been breached. This suggests that, in addition to being a poor forecaster, it is also lax in controlling the cash flow within the business. Poor cash control within a business is one of the most common reasons for business failure – even for businesses that are profitable[6].

It is perfectly normally for a business to have an "in case of need" overdraft facility. Much like the SAL used for personal customers this facility allow a business to manage the small timing differences of income and expenditure and to smooth out the variations of sales/income which occur in every business. Generally in case of need facilities will be reviewed annually. As with SALs, the limit should not be automatically renewed without a number of steps being taken.

1.   The business should provide the up-to-date accounts.[7]

2.   The customer should be meet – preferably at the business premises.

3.   The swing on the account should be reviewed. Is there a hard-core position developing?

As with personal customers, it may be necessary to capitalize the hard core onto a loan

---

[6]   This is not a mistake or misprint. Profitable businesses have often gone into liquidation because of poor cash management.
[7]   We shall look at analysing these in Chapters 4 and 5.

account. Of which more soon.

Before leaving revolving credit we need to look at credit cards and charge cards. Look at the table below.

Credit and charge cards

Table 3.6

Limit	Payments made	Credits received	Balance	Available credit
500			nil	500
	15		15 dr.	485
	25		40 dr.	460
	250		290 dr.	210
	150		440 dr.	60
		440	0	500

In this situation the entire debit balance has been repaid. This is a defining characteristic of charge cards. In credit cards you would see the following.

Table 3.7

Limit	Payments made	Credits received	Balance	Available credit
500				500
	15		15 dr.	485
	25		40 dr.	460
	250		290 dr.	210
	150		440 dr.	60
		22	418 dr.	72
Interest	4.40		422.40 dr.	77.60

With the credit card the customer is not under any obligation to repay the entire overdrawn balance at once. The normal commitment is a payment of either 3% or 5% of the outstanding balance. Interest will be charged on the outstanding balance, although most credit cards give customers extended interest-free credit of upto to 56 days. Thus those who clear off the debit balance within the 56 days pay no interest.

Neither credit nor charge cards should be confused with debit cards. The debit card is purely an electronic method of money transmission. It simply allows access to funds in the account of the cardholder.

To summarize – revolving credit accounts involve the balance on the account fluctuating between a maximum debit balance and either a zero or a credit balance.

These types of account are ideal for cash-flow management and are utilized by literally millions of people every day. Some would argue that the growth of such facilities has pandered to the greed that we all experience. Others counter this by saying that the facility is purely a tool. How that tool is used is not the province of the toolmaker. Is a gunmaker responsible if the gun kills a man?[8]

You should not consider the ethics of lending for the purposes of the examination, but as your career progresses this aspect will become more important.

One thing is certain for all revolving-credit accounts. They are not a suitable medium for high-value asset purchase needing to be repaid over several years. The main reason for this is the high interest rates levied by the card providers.

Research time – compare the interest rates charged by your employer on revolving credit with the rate it charges on loan accounts.

3.3 Loan accounts

A loan account is normally requested to facilitate the larger expenditure. This falls into short/medium-term and long-term. Under the short/medium-term scenario we would expect loan periods of between 12 months and 7 years. There are number of possible requests in this timeframe. These might include:

- *car purchase*

    - Probably the most common reason for the request of a loan. The average new family car costs in excess of £10,000 and will certainly be the second largest purchase most people make. Given that the average salary in the UK is approximately £18,000 it is obvious that the car will not be paid for with the normal span of an overdraft.

        However, the first car purchased is rarely a brand new model. Consequently the level of loan will be less and repayment is usually accomplished within a few years.

- *time share purchase*

    The purchase of a week's accommodation, at a certain place, in perpetuity. This week can then be swapped for other locations worldwide. Why might somebody do something like this? For a one-off payment – often measured in the region of £5,000 to £10,000 – the purchaser effectively pays the bulk of holiday costs for the remainder of his or her lifetime. Although expensive now, this cuts costs in the future. Is this an

---

[8] Several court cases are pending in the USA on just this point.

acceptable loan purpose? An alternative could be to purchase a caravan – touring or static. The advantage of the caravan scenario would be the availability of tangible security but the principles are the same.

The car and the timeshare show that loans can be for real asset purchase (car) and virtual asset purchase (timeshare). In both cases ability to repay the loan is the fundamental consideration. And the key to repayment is cash flow.

- *stocks and shares*

    A little different from cars and caravans, stocks and shares fall into the category of financial assets.[9] Here the purchase always has an element of risk – the risk of the asset falling very quickly to zero value. A car will depreciate in value but can maintain its usefulness as a car for 10 to 15 years. It can be insured against fire, theft, etc. You cannot insure against the fall of a share price. Generally speaking, lending for share purchase is deemed to be lending to gamble and would fall outside the normal lending criteria. Occasionally a customer might need/wish to take up rights under a rights issue[10]. This request may be granted although often on an overdraft. As will be seen in Chapter 8, stocks and shares can make suitable security.

- *home improvements*

    A very common request. Here the applicant is looking for assistance to cover the cost of refurbishment to the home, e.g. central heating/double glazing/extension.

- *debt consolidation*

    Again a common request. Our driving force of greed coupled with the impetus of a "have now" society lead many people to borrow money from several different sources at the same time.

    If you walk down the high street you will see advertisements in every shop window for the in-house credit card and practically anybody can pick up £5,000 to £10,000 worth of credit very quickly. (Just trust me on this – do not go and try it.) The terms of the cards seem fine – pay back 3% or 5% or the indebtedness per month.

    Sadly many people end up with three or four credit cards, a few store cards and a monthly servicing cost of more than they can afford. Combining the debts (which invariably will be at high interest rates) onto one loan spread over a longer timeframe combined with a lower rate of interest can save a customer pounds. The main considerations for the lender are:

    - can the customer afford the new payments?
    - is this a regular occurrence?

Obviously once the credit card debts have been repaid (taken out) the customer has full use of the revolving credit within the credit/store card again. And could fall into the temptation of spend, spend, spend again. While this phenomena was reasonable common in the 70s

---

[9] We look more at types of assets in Chapter 8.

[10] Companies wishing to raise finance often use existing shareholders and give them the opportunity to invest more in the company by buying extra shares (on a pro rata basis) at a discounted cost, e.g. buy £10,000 worth of extra shares for £8,500.

and 80s – it was not unheard of to take a credit card from a customer – it is less likely now. However, careful monitoring of the current account should be undertaken – especially at SAL review – to see if there is evidence of credit-card indebtedness building up. A key sign is the existence of regular cheques for round amounts. Most of the goods we buy have prices like £X. 49 or £X.99. Most credit card bills are the same (based on 3%/5%) but research has shown that most people round up the payment to a credit card company to the nearest pound (or five pounds).

Lending for debt consolidation is not, in and of itself, bad or dangerous. The problem may perhaps have been caused by a period of unemployment or illness. However, repeated requests to take out the debts of other lenders should be viewed with caution.

In each of the above examples (and there are many more acceptable reasons – look at your employer's loan applications forms for further possibilities), the loan facility will be for between 12 months and seven years. The lender will usually have two loan facilities. The first is where interest is charged on a reducing-balance basis and the second where the interest is charged up-front on the entire amount borrowed. For example, in the first scenario a loan of £3,000 is approved over three years at an interest rate of 10%. The interest is charged monthly and capital is repaid in equal instalments.

Thus:

$$3,000/36 = 83.33 \text{ capital repayments per month}$$

$$3,000 \times 10\%/12 = 25.00$$

A first monthly payment of £108.33 will cover the interest and reduce the outstanding debt by £83.33 and thus reduce the interest due in Month 2. Over the 36 months we have a repayment profile as follows:

Table 3.8

Debt	Interest	Payment	Balance	
3000	25	3025	-108.33	2916.67
2916.67	24.30558	2940.976	-107.636	2833.34
2833.34	23.61117	2856.951	-106.941	2750.01
2750.01	22.91675	2772.927	-106.247	2666.68
2666.68	22.22233	2688.902	-105.552	2583.35
2583.35	21.52792	2604.878	-104.858	2500.02
2500.02	20.8335	2520.854	-104.164	2416.69
2416.69	20.13908	2436.829	-103.469	2333.36
2333.36	19.44467	2352.805	-102.775	2250.03
2250.03	18.75025	2268.78	-102.08	2166.7
2166.7	18.05583	2184.756	-101.386	2083.37
2083.37	17.36142	2100.731	-100.691	2000.04
2000.04	16.667	2016.707	-99.997	1916.71
1916.71	15.97258	1932.683	-99.3026	1833.38
1833.38	15.27817	1848.658	-98.6082	1750.05
1750.05	14.58375	1764.634	-97.9138	1666.72
1666.72	13.88933	1680.609	-97.2193	1583.39
1583.39	13.19492	1596.585	-96.5249	1500.06
1500.06	12.5005	1512.561	-95.8305	1416.73
1416.73	11.80608	1428.536	-95.1361	1333.4
1333.4	11.11167	1344.512	-94.4417	1250.07
1250.07	10.41725	1260.487	-93.7473	1166.74
1166.74	9.722833	1176.463	-93.0528	1083.41
1083.41	9.028417	1092.438	-92.3584	1000.08
1000.08	8.334	1008.414	-91.664	916.75
916.75	7.639583	924.3896	-90.9696	833.42
833.42	6.945167	840.3652	-90.2752	750.09
750.09	6.25075	756.3408	-89.5808	666.76

Debt	Interest	Payment	Balance	
666.76	5.556333	672.3163	-88.8863	583.43
583.43	4.861917	588.2919	-88.1919	500.1
500.1	4.1675	504.2675	-87.4975	416.77
416.77	3.473083	420.2431	-86.8031	333.44
333.44	2.778667	336.2187	-86.1087	250.11
250.11	2.08425	252.1943	-85.4143	166.78
166.78	1.389833	168.1698	-84.7198	83.45
83.45	0.695417	84.14542	-84.0254	0.12

If you total the interest charged you should get to £462.52. The debt outstanding is 12 pence. For marketing purposes the monthly repayment will be calculated as a regular payment.

The major drawback of this method is that the customer is at the mercy of rising interest rates although they would benefit from any interest-rate cuts.

With Scenario 2 the interest for the entire period is calculated up-front and repayments calculated on the capital plus entire interest divided by the number of months. In effect the interest rate is fixed up-front. In risk management terms "interest rate risk has been transferred to the lender". If rates rise the lender must bear the cost of this. Usually lenders will make use of derivatives known as interest rate swaps to reduce the risk to themselves. In-depth study of the field of derivatives is a few years away.

The costing works thus:

$3,000 \times 10\% \times 3 = 900 + 3,000 = 3,900$ divided by $36 = 108.33$

This gives the following repayment profile:

Table 3.9

Debt	Payment	Balance
3900	-108.33	3791.67
3791.67	-108.33	3683.34
3683.34	-108.33	3575.01
3575.01	-108.33	3466.68
3466.68	-108.33	3358.35
3358.35	-108.33	3250.02
3250.02	-108.33	3141.69
3141.69	-108.33	3033.36
3033.36	-108.33	2925.03
2925.03	-108.33	2816.7
2816.7	-108.33	2708.37
2708.37	-108.33	2600.04
2600.04	-108.33	2491.71
2491.71	-108.33	2383.38
2383.38	-108.33	2275.05
2275.05	-108.33	2166.72
2166.72	-108.33	2058.39
2058.39	-108.33	1950.06
1950.06	-108.33	1841.73
1841.73	-108.33	1733.4
1733.4	-108.33	1625.07
1625.07	-108.33	1516.74
1516.74	-108.33	1408.41
1408.41	-108.33	1300.08
1300.08	-108.33	1191.75
1191.75	-108.33	1083.42
1083.42	-108.33	975.09
975.09	-108.33	866.76

Debt	Payment	Balance	
866.76	-108.33	758.43	
758.43	-108.33	650.1	
650.1	-108.33	541.77	
541.77	-108.33	433.44	
433.44	-108.33	325.11	
325.11	-108.33	216.78	
216.78	-108.33	108.45	
108.45	-108.33	0.12	

A couple of points to note:

1. The final debt is 12p. In both case this will be adjusted in the first or last payment.

2. The total interest paid by the customer is £900. This equates to almost 95% more interest to the lender for the same amount of loan over the same period.

3. In the event of an early settlement of the debt the Consumer Credit Act 1974[11] provides for a refund of the unearned interest.

4) If the borrower under Scenario 1 paid the same £108.33 as the borrower in Scenario 2, then the debt would be repaid in 31, as opposed to 36, months.

Obviously the personal loan favours the lender as opposed to the borrower in this form of lending.

Before leaving the section loosely covered under the heading medium-term loans, we could usefully consider the *probate loan*.

Probate loan

When a person dies his or her financial estate is assessed as to its overall value. If the estate is being left entirely to a surviving spouse there is no tax to pay at any level. However, if the estate is not left to a spouse, only amounts up to £231,000 (99/00) are passed to the heirs without deduction of tax. Any amount in excess of the *inheritance tax threshold* will be taxed at 40%. Under current English law the inheritance tax must be paid to the Inland Revenue before any distribution to the beneficiaries. This can often cause problems. Take the following situation.

[11] Of which more later.

Uncle Fred has passed away leaving the following assets:

	£
House	200,000
Stocks and shares	150,000
Gilts	150,000
Bank account	10,000
Total estate	510,000
IHT threshold	231,000
Taxable estate	279,000
Tax due	111,600

Assume that the will appoints you as executor. It is your responsibility to pay this £111,600 to the Inland Revenue. The chances are that you have not got that type of cash available. You cannot sell part of the assets to pay the bill. What to do? You seek a probate loan. There are two possible sources for this facility.

1. Your bank – it will know you but will take convincing of the value of the estate.

2. The deceased's bank – it will probably know the value of the estate but probably not you.

Despite the disadvantages inherent in both choices, you will almost certainly be granted the facility. The main consideration is the type of loan. This will depend on the structure of the estate. In our example the facility will be very short-term. As soon as the tax liability has been discharged you will be able to effect repayment from the sale of shares or gilts. In a different scenario the figures might be the same but the estate made up of a house worth £500,000 and £10,000 in cash. Selling the house could take longer or the beneficiaries might wish to live in the house. In this case they would need to raise a mortgage loan on the property to repay the probate loan.

Long-term loans

Long-term loans are generally for property purchase and, as you are probably aware, such facilities are called *mortgages*. We will discuss the appropriateness (or otherwise) of the term mortgage is this context in Chapters 6 and 7.

Mortgage lending falls into two categories. The first is the repayment mortgage[12]. In this type of mortgage the monthly repayment consists of interest and capital. No lender, *anywhere*, uses the personal loan method of interest calculation. Indeed lenders are currently falling over themselves to let customers know how fairly they calculate interest. Some new entrants to the financial services field are even promoting accounts that combine the current account and the repayment mortgage. The theory is that the revolving credit aspect of the current

---

[12] Also called capital and interest mortgage.

account reduces the interest charge for a few days every month, thus reducing the interest charged.

Imagine for a moment that 25 years interest on a £50,000 mortgage was added to the loan up-front!

The second repayment method for property purchase is *interest-only*. In this case the debt remains unchanged throughout the term of the loan and the debt is the same at the end of the loan period as at the beginning. The debt is technically repaid by a 'bullet' repayment at the end. This 'bullet' is normally generated from an endowment policy, pension plan or ISA.[13]

As well as two repayment alternatives the customer will also be able to choose from a range of interest-rate charging profiles.

Variable rates

This rate fluctuates to reflect changes in the external market place and is heavily influenced by government policy and the Monetary Policy Committee. All overdraft and other revolving credit facilities are charged at the variable rate. As discussed previously, ordinary loans are charged this way. Borrowers convinced of the continued downward trend in market rates will seek to have all the borrowing at variable rates.

Fixed rates

For those who are uncertain of the future direction of rates then the option to fix a rate for a set time period is attractive. The main advantage is in budgeting. If you fix the rate at 10% for five years, you know exactly what the facility cost will be for that period. Borrowers with memories of the late 1980s and early 1990s (when mortgage rates rose to over 15%) are very fond of the certainty and stability such fixing brings.

Capped rates

This combines the advantages of the variable rate with the security of budgeting seen with fixed rates. Here the lender sets a maximum interest rate but the rate charge will move below that maximum if variable rates move down. This option is often restricted to certain types of borrowers. Normally this will be those with good equity levels in their property.

Capped and collared rates

You have probably noticed that with the capped rate the interest rate risk is transferred solely to the lender. In the capped/collar variant the lender sets a maximum rate it will charge and, additionally, set a minimum rate that will be paid by the borrower.

Discounted rate

Here the variable rate is reduced by a fixed discount.

The fixed, capped, capped/collared and discount options normally apply to the loan for a set period of up to five years.

---

[13] ISAs replaced PEPs in April 1999 and the PEP mortgage disappeared.

As you are aware, the mortgage market is by far the most competitive within the financial services industry at the moment[14]. Accordingly all lenders have simplified the process as much as possible. The lending criteria have essentially been reduced to three main considerations.

1. Can the borrower afford the repayments? In an effort to simplify this there is a historical set of formulas utilized by most lenders. This is based on the salary multiplier.

    The most common multipliers are:

    > 3 times the primary salary plus the secondary

    > or

    > 2.5 times the joint salary.

    Many lenders have variations on this theme. *What does your employer use?*

    Example:

    > Fred and Sally want to buy a house. Fred earns £12,000 per annum and Sally earns £26,000. Their borrowing potential is therefore either

    > $(26,000 \times 3) + 12,000 = 90,000$

    > or

    > $(26,000 + 12,000) \times 2.5 = 95,000$

    Many commentators have been suggesting recently that while such a simple format was useful in the past, changes must be considered for today. Specifically, interest rates today (and arguably for the foreseeable future) are very low[15] and most people now have other loans in addition to a mortgage.

    With these consideration in mind perhaps a more detailed analysis of affordability should be considered.

2. *Value of Security*: Domestic property has historically been seen as among the better forms of security. And even after the property slump of the late 1980s and early 1990s this type of security is still considered to be extremely stable.

3) *Amount of Equity*: Or how much of their own money are Fred and Sally using as a deposit. If the couple are first-time buyers then most lenders will lend them up to 95% of the purchase price provided;

    *   The overall loan is not more than £95,000 – this equates to a purchase price of £100,000

    *   A report and valuation from an approved valuer confirming that the property is suitable security for a loan of £95,000. Please note that this does not confirm that the £100,000 being paid is a fair price.

---

[14] Closely followed by credit cards.
[15] When viewed historically.

At a loan to value (LTV) of 95% (loan divided by value), the lender usually seeks additional security in the form of a *mortgage guarantee indemnity policy* (MGIP)[16]. Essentially this is a guarantee provided by an insurance company. The terms are normally such that if Fred and Sally default and the lender is forced to repossess the property then the insurance company will make good any losses of the lender. Much has been made in the press (and in some court cases) of the right of subrogation which the insurance company possesses. This enabls the insurer to claim any payments to the lender from the owner of the repossessed property – even though it is the customer who has paid for the cost of the insurance.

Bridging loans

We cannot leave study of facilities for property purchase without considering *bridging loans*. The general timetable for property transactions is:

1. Decide to sell existing property.

2. Look for new property.

3. Make offer on new property/agree to sell existing – not necessarily contemporaneously.

4. Solicitor arranges for sale and purchase to take place on the same day.

Stage 4 allows for the equity in the existing property to be rolled into the new purchase.

Example

Mr and Mrs Price are moving. Their current home is being sold for £85,000 and their existing mortgage is £50,000. The proposed new home is £100,000 and their existing lender has agreed to lend them £65,000.

The following occurs:

Cash In	85,000	– from sale
Cash out	50,000	– repay mortgage
Balance	35,000	– the equity
Cash in	65,000	– new mortgage
Cash out	100,000	– purchase new property
Balance	NIL	

In reality the existing may not be repaid and drawdown of a new loan of £15,000 will enable the transaction to proceed.

Occasionally it will appear that the sale and purchase are not going to be contemporaneous. This might be due to a number of factors, of which the most common of which are

a) The buyer dropping out before exchange of contacts.

b) The buyer being unable to complete until a later date.

[16] Many lenders call this MGI or MIP.

The options available to Mr and Mrs Price are limited. They can forget the whole transaction. This would be the norm. Or they can take a bridging loan. Here their lender lends them the equity in addition to the £65,000. This extra amount will be repaid when their existing property is sold.

Granting of bridging loans by lenders is a difficult decision. By implication, the customer must be creditworthy or the mortgage facility would not have been granted. Therefore what reasons might there be for not granting the bridging loan?

a) The customer will be paying interest on the long-term loan and on the bridging loan. Can their cash flow manage this? The only way around this is to allow interest to roll up unpaid on the bridging loan. This increases the debt by approximately £400 per month.[17]

b) When will the existing property be sold? – Is the sale certain? Bridging loans are either *closed* – the selling date has been agreed and evidenced by a legally binding exchange of contracts – or open – there is no fixed date or even buyer. An open bridge is more difficult to approve because the repayment date is not known and the amount of equity is impossible to calculate. Mr and Mrs Price may need to reduce the selling price to £80,000 and the property may not sell for twelve months. If interest has not been met there is an extra £4,750 to pay. To balance the equation Mr and Mrs Price will need to borrow an extra £9,750 as a mortgage loan.

Some lenders do not entertain any form of bridging finance. Others lend on short-term closed bridges only. Only a few lenders entertain open-ended bridging loans.

3.4   Business borrowing

What have we covered so far?

1. Revolving credits

> Overdrafts

>> Salary anticipatory limits ⎫
>>
>> ⎬ For personal customers
>>
>> Specific need limits ⎭

>> In case of need ⎫
>>
>> ⎬ For business customers
>>
>> Trading facilities ⎭

>> Credit cards   Liquidity needs/desires

2. Personal loans   Asset purchase medium-term

3. Ordinary loans   Asset purchase medium-term

[17] £50,000 x 9.5 %/12- this rate reflects 4 % above base rate in early 1999.

4. Probate loans	Pay inheritance tax – short-term
5. Mortgage loans	House purchase – long term

As you review the above you will see that we have focused primarily on the needs of the personal customer. Do businesses not need to borrow? Obviously they do. And to partly agree with the bank official quoted at the beginning of the chapter, their needs are roughly the same as personal customers.

The majority of businesses require a working overdraft facility for day-to-day cash-flow management. They may also need to borrow funds over the medium[18] and longer terms for asset purchase. As with personal borrowers the lender generally links the period with the expected useful lifetime of the asset up to certain maximums. These maximums vary from lender to lender but generally medium-term will be up to seven years, with long-term property purchase being limited to fifteen years.

However there are a few special facilities which are often requested by, and made available to, businesses.

1. New business start-up funds.

2. Business expansion.

3. Stocking loans.

4. Plant and machinery purchase.

5. Factoring.

6. Hire purchase and leasing.

7. Franchising.

8. Small firms loan guarantee scheme.

These facilities can be made available by either overdraft or loan but the initial application for the facilities needs to be supported by a *business plan*. Indeed it would be fair to say:

> *No business plan. No facility.*

The business plan

Essentially the business plan is a quantitative and qualitative assessment of where the business is and where it is going. It should include the following elements.

Qualitative

1. CVs of the directors and key personnel.

2. Details of the product line.

3. Details of the location of the business.

[18] A little aside – businesses do not have the interest front-end loaded to their medium-term loans.

4. Details of the market.

5. Details of the competitors.

6. Plans and objectives of the business.

7. Strategies for achieving these plans and objectives.

Items 4 to 7 are normally dealt with together in a *SWOT analysis*.

A SWOT analysis looks at the following aspects of a business:

Strengths

It is useful for a business to correctly ascertain what its main strengths are. This section should consider internal strengths (management, cash flow, location, etc.) and external strengths, i.e. What does the business do better than its competitors?

Weaknesses

As important as discerning strengths is discovering and acknowledging the weaknesses – again both internal and external. The primary reason is to enable a strategy for dealing with them to be formulated. You are aware that a chain is only as strong as its weakest link; similarly a business is only as strong as its weakest area. Examples of internal weaknesses might be in cash-flow management or marketing skills. Once identified these can often be overcome by hiring people who possess the requisite skills.

An external weakness might be a poor location compared with a competitor. This might mean that transport costs (and delivery times) are greater than the competitor's. Once identified a number of solutions should be considered. These could be moving – drastic but perhaps necessary – or consideration of alternative transport methods (rail as opposed to road). The essential caveat to considering weaknesses is that they are not to be ignored. It might well be that no changes are made due to cost/benefit analysis considerations but the inaction should be based on decisiveness, not ignorance. It is almost certain that competitors will be analysing the weaknesses within competitors and seeking strategies to exploit them.

The failure to have identified weaknesses is in itself a weakness, and should be viewed with scepticism. It would suggest a weakness in management competence.

Opportunities

Often it is the identification of business opportunities that will have been the catalyst for the requested facility. The option to buy the shop unit next door might be an opportunity for this business to expand its selling space cheaply. The business will need to show that utilizing the opportunity will be financially viable.

Threats

These are elements that might harm a business. For example, to a dress manufacturer a major threat is changing fashion tastes. For an established financial institution, the current threat is the growth of financial services offered by companies such as Sainsburys, Marks and Spencer and Virgin. It will be interesting to see how Barclays, etc. respond[19].

The table below is by no means complete. It is not even extensive. Different businesses will have different types of SWOTs.

Table 3.10

Possible Strengths	Potential Weaknesses
Competent management	Out-of-date production techniques
Good financial resources	Poor management
Good brand awareness	Narrow product range
Acknowledged product superiority	Under-capitalization
Good marketing skills	Poor staff relations
Advanced technical skills	Poor distribution network
Opportunities	**Threats**
Complacency of rivals	New rules and regulations
New technologies	Business cycle
Export possibilities	Changing taste of customers
Flexible technology	Demographic changes

All the qualitative information must be supported by the figures. A business owner might suggest that buying the unit next door is an unmissable opportunity for his business to grow. If, however, the balance sheet shows static sales and falling profit margins, the prudent lender would want to know how taking on an extra expense will help the business.

Quantitative

1. Historical accounts

2. Forecast profit and loss and balance sheets

3. Cash-flow forecasts

We shall look at all of the above in Chapter 4.

As stated earlier every lender will insist on a business plan in support of requests for facilities. Having looked at the business plan, let us refresh our memory of the type of request that would usually require one to be prepared.

[19] Beans for sale in the banking hall?

New business start-up

This is by far the most difficult of propositions brought before a lender. While several of the elements are fairly simply to confirm (stake injected by directors, for example), most factors are conjecture. It is impossible, for example, to say with any degree of certainty what the level of sales will be.

Business expansion

You are moving into an easier area here. Business expansion falls into two main categories. Firstly businesses may want to expand capacity to sell more of a successful product. The existing financial data may show increasing sales and profitability. The second scenario might be business expansion by way of diversification. A company selling product "A" might well decide that a new product, "B", should be introduced and developed on the strength of product "A". Indeed product "B" might be the successor of "A", whose lifespan is coming to an end.

Both the above scenarios could utilize the overdraft and term loan facilities.

Stocking loans

Here, as the term suggests, the lender is lending to enable a business to purchase stock. This is certainly a difficult situation, although often seen in relation to international trade. Generally speaking, a business should be able to generate sufficient cash flow to restock as necessary. A possible scenario could be to enable a builder to purchase land which it will subsequently develop and sell. Another possible scenario would be an antiques dealer who wishes to buy a particular piece for which he already has a buyer. Here a short-term increase in an overdraft facility might be granted.

The lender may well agree to the stocking facility to generate cash to reduce an unsatisfactory position.

Take our builder. The firm owes £100,000 which is hard core. The opportunity has arisen to purchase a plot of land for £20,000. The builder can build four properties on the land at a cost of £40,000 each and sell them at £100,000 each.[20]

Stocking loan	100,000	
Build cost[21]	160,000	
	260,000	
Selling price	400,000	
Gross profit	140,000	
Expenses	*say* 25,000	
Net profit	115,000	this would go to reducing the overdraft.

[20] Saleability and price confirmed by independent valuer.
[21] Via stage payments.

Plant and machinery purchase

This is a common request, although one that should be viewed with caution. As with stock, a business should be generating sufficient funds to replace equipment that wears out or becomes obsolete. Indeed every business will be depreciating[22] the value of these assets. The amount of depreciation is treated as if the business had spent the money and reduces the tax due *but does not leave the business*. Thus there *should*, theoretically, be sufficient reserves within a business to fund normal replacement. In practice, however, this is not always the case. This could be for several reasons – new unexpected technologies making plant obsolete, wrong depreciation period or method chosen or, as is often the case, the business is utilizing capital elsewhere. The key considerations with stocking facilities are cash flow and life span. You would not lend £10,000 over fifteen years to buy some equipment that has to be replaced in five years.

It is possible that each of the four facilities discussed above will require some form of security. Often this proves to be a stumbling block in start-up situations or young businesses. In order to overcome these problems, the Department of Trade and Industry will provide the security to the lender by the way of either the *Small Firms Loan Guarantee Scheme* (SFLGS) or the *Small Loans Arrangement Scheme* (SLAS). These loans (and the guarantees) are typically for between two and seven years and are only made available for new borrowing. The major restriction is in relation to buying into a company or partnership. As a further assistance the facilities can be made available via capital repayment holidays. The loan will be with a lender and interest needs to be negotiated as normal.

Look at the table below.

Table 3.11

	SFLGS	SLAS
Percent of guarantee		
New businesses	70%	70%
Established business	85%	85%
Amount of guarantee		
New	5000-100000	5000-30000
Established	5000-250000	5000-30000
DTI premium		
Fixed interest rate	0.5 %	0.5 %
Variable rate	1.5 %	1.5%
Capital repayment holiday	Max. 24 months	6, 12 or 24 months
Drawdown	Instalments	Lump sum

[22] Reducing: see Chapter 4.

Thus a new business seeking a loan to purchase a retail outlet could receive a loan guarantee of up to 70% of the purchase price (up to £100,000) and make no capital repayments for two years. This obviously helps the venture to bed down. From a lender's point of view it has been able to lend to a viable project which would otherwise have been rejected for lack of security.

Factoring

Limited companies will normally need to extend credit to their customers. For regular customers this may eventually be a form of revolving credit. While the customer owes money he is a debtor. Unfortunately, while debtors are part of the current assets of a business, they cannot be spent. They can, however, be factored. A factoring company is a specialized financial institution (although often they are subsidiaries of major groups) that advances funds to a company against the level of the debts. For example, if the debts for the month are £250,000, the factor might give a facility of 75%. This releases £187,500 immediately into the company, thus reducing its reliance on overdraft facilities. This percentage will depend on the quality of the company and the quality of the debtors. Any company owed money by me is less likely to be able to factor it than if the company was owed by British Telecom. Normally the factor will want the *debtor book* to be widespread and active. The debts will be collected and the factor, and his charge, paid.

Hire purchase and leasing

These are alternatives to outright, immediate purchase of assets. In return for an initial payment, the borrower gets the use of the asset but not ownership. During the period of the agreement payments are made to the lender for the continued right to use. With hire purchase, ownership passes to the customer with a compulsory final payment whereas with leasing the final payment is optional and if not exercised the asset is returned. Many car dealerships are offering lease-style contracts to encourage us to buy new cars. In this case we can take possession of, and have use of, the new car. At the end of the period we can either:

- pay the final payment and drive away;
- enter into a new contract for a new car;
- park the old car on the forecourt and drive away.

As with factoring these facilities are offered by specialized institutions. Again these institutions are often subsidiaries of the major finance groups.

Franchising

This occurs where the owner of a successful business expands, not by the traditional means of opening more outlets and employing more staff, but by selling the right to use the business name and idea in a specific area to a third party. In return for a franchise fee, the third party gets a proven idea, product or brand together with the expertise of the franchisor in running the business. In addition, he or she may well benefit from national advertising and promotions.

Probably the most successful franchise in the world is Mcdonalds. The advantages should be obvious. The purchaser of the franchise has all the existing marketing and brand loyalty behind him or her from day one. He or she has the in-built supplier chains. In return for providing these advantages and ongoing support and marketing, the franchisor will receive either a percentage of the profits or a fixed annual fee – or both.

Lending to buy into a franchise can be good business for a lender. The basic idea will be tried and tested. The normal pitfalls and dangers are often avoided – having already been overcome by the franchisor. Statistics suggest that franchise businesses are far more likely to succeed than stand-alone start-up situations. This does not, however, mean that the normal lending considerations are ignored. Consideration of the standard criteria still needs to be undertaken, and passed.

The other side of the coin is when a customer is seeking to franchise his existing business. Although the business is successful, it is probable that the customer will require specialized assistance both in terms of finance and experience to launch a successful franchise. There are numerous magazines with details of established franchise availability. It would do you no harm to buy one and see how many household names are, in fact, franchisees. You will also see advertisements from a wide variety of financial institutions offering support.

Monitoring facilities

Having granted the requested facility (of whatever nature) we must not be complacent. Efficient and effective monitoring of lending is the best way to reduce bad debts because it reduces the number and value of loans a lender must write off against profits.

Essentially monitoring is an easy procedure. With loans accounts a simple check that the monthly payment has been received will suffice. Overdrafts are harder to monitor.

It might well be that the overdraft is within its limit but the limit might easily be hiding problems. How can we spot these?

Compare with the cash flow forecasts

A current account balance is not expected to agree with the forecasted closing bank balance exactly. The very nature of forecasting and business makes that an impossibility. However a discrepancy of more than 10% may require further consideration.

Is a hard-core position developing?

A reduction in swing on a current account is always a clear sign that problems are beginning to surface. This may need to be corrected by a capital injection or by setting up a loan account. Certainly the lender will want to speak to the customer and look at the current trading position. This usually involves looking at the management accounts of the business concerned. Lack of such accounts would be a real warning sign because this would suggest weak management.

Breaching of the overdraft limit

Most financial institutions have some form of out-of-order report. This report provides a list of accounts that will be overdrawn in excess of agreed limits at the close of business. The lending officer needs to ascertain what items will cause the breach (some reports incorporate this information) and make a judgement as to what action to take. Possible causes of a breach include:

- *Cheque* – Is this within the cheque-card limit? If it is, then payment must be made to the payee. If not then consideration should be given to returning the cheque.

- *Standing order/direct debit* – Neither of these is covered by the cheque guarantee provisions so the lender is well within its rights to return.

Once the out-of-order position has been identified then consideration must be given as to how this might be regularized. This can be achieved by either returning (bouncing) a debit or having funds paid in to bring the account within the limit.

Before returning a cheque or standing order the following steps should be considered:

- Has the customer contacted you or a colleague advising of the breach and making an agreement to restore the out-of-order position?

- What damage will bouncing do to the customer's creditworthiness and reputation in the world at large?

- What is the debit for? It does no good to return a payment to a loan account the customer has with you.

- Does the customer have credit balances on other accounts which can be set off? For example, if a customer has £10,000 in a deposit, it would be foolhardy to bounce a cheque for £150.

- Is the customer the managing director of your largest customer or a partner in a major professional firm that banks with you?

- Can the customer be contacted? Never return an item without making every effort to speak to the customer. Obviously take care here. If the account concerned is a sole account do not tell a partner (even if they have a joint account) of the position. When contacting a customer at work be *very* discrete. Do not leave a message with a receptionist asking Fred to phone you about his overdraft! The advantage of contacting the customer is twofold. The customer may be aware of the breach and is arranging for funds to be paid in to correct it. The breach may be a simple oversight and the customer will again organize funds to be paid in later in the day.

  The second benefit is that if the customer has no explanation for the excess and offers no plans to regularize the situation you can tell the customer that you will be returning the item. This leaves the customer in no doubt as to your proposed action and will often change his or her position. Even if it does not, then at least the customer has a chance to warn the payee and attempt to limit the damage.

If the customer cannot be contacted, you will need to inspect the branch records. Have items been returned before? If not, it would strongly suggest that you consult with a colleague before making the decision to return. Although returning the cheque will regularize the account it will also result in a number of other consequences. Firstly the hitherto elusive customer will suddenly appear. Secondly the action will have stated your intent to control the account. Thirdly you may lose the account – and any associated accounts.

Consideration of the various legends on returned items are not part of this course but:

Research time again – go and find out.

Are there signs of cross firing?

This is when the current account has credits being paid in to stop the breach of an overdraft limit followed in a few days with a payment to another financial institution. Effectively the customer is playing one lender off against the other by making use of the cheque clearing cycle. Cross-fired cheques are often for round amounts. This can often hide deep-seated financial problems and needs to be addressed quickly.

Is there evidence of overtrading?

This problem is specifically seen with business customers. The clearest sign is an unexplained rise in both credit and debit turnover on an account. While on the face of things the increase in sales might seem a good thing – *"more sales more profit"* – often the business is selling faster than it can produce or restock, or selling more because of a decrease in prices. Although the business might be within its overdraft limit care should be exercised. Those who run before they can walk properly invariably fall over. If overtrading appears a possibility, ask the customer for sight of the management accounts. If debtor days, creditor days and stock turnover are rising and gross margins are falling then overtrading is almost certainly happening. The best cure for this is to increase the capital in the business and/or restructure the facilities offered to the business.

Although unpleasant, it is often necessary to return items to control the spending of those who cannot control their own. If we do not then we will end up with a doubtful debt and eventually a bad debt. These are both failures for lenders because they represent lost money (which was not the lender's in the first place) and lost profit, which reduces the returns for investors in the lender. Have a look at the effect of bad debts on the balance sheets of the UK clearing banks in the early 1990s. So what are these doubtful debts and bad debts?

- *doubtful debts* are those amounts owed that in the judgement of the lender may not be repaid in full;

- *bad debts* are those amounts owing that will definitely not be paid.

Once a doubtful debt has been identified, action must be taken to recover all (or as much as possible) of the debt. There are a number of stages in this recovery process.

Preliminary action

This is usually by means of a formal letter to a customer requesting repayment of the debt within a specified timescale. It will also advise the customer of the potential remedies and actions open to the lender.

Agreed settlement

After receipt of the above letter the customer often makes a proposal to repay some or all of the debt immediately or by instalments. If the customer makes such a proposal it should be treated very seriously. The prime aim is to get the debt repaid not sue the customer. Legal action is always expensive.

Garnishee order

If the customer refuses to respond to the formal demand, or reneges on an agreed settlement, the option of a garnishee order should be considered. This order, granted by the court, freezes all the bank accounts of the debtor in the UK and enables repayment to be made from the other bank accounts. This does presuppose that such accounts exist and are in credit.

Prior to starting any court action the lesson of "blood and stones" needs to be considered.

Attachment of earnings order

This is useful if the debtor has a regular income from a job but no capital. If the court approves an attachment order, a set amount will be deducted directly from the debtor's salary before he or she receives it.

Mareva injunction

This is used when a lender suspects that debtor is about to dispose of assets which could otherwise be used to repay the debt. The mareva injunction acts as a restraining order which prevents the aforementioned sale.

Charging order

Normally this is for larger debts. The court allows a legal charge to be placed on assets of the debtor. This means that when the asset is sold, funds must be remitted to the lender to discharge the debt before the asset owner receives the funds (see Chapters 6, 7 and 8).

Execution of assets

Here the court orders that the assets to be sold to repay the indebtedness.

Bankruptcy proceedings

We considered the effects of bankruptcy earlier and will say nothing extra except that this action is a last resort. In the case of a company, liquidation not bankruptcy proceedings would be started.

When starting on any of the above courses of action, the debt would be doubtful. If these methods fail then the debt is bad.

4

FINANCIAL STATEMENTS

Every business needs to know how well it has performed over a particular time period. In order to do this every business produces, each year, a set of financial statements.

These statements are all based on a set of basic accounting concepts which we should spend some time considering.

The fundamental accounting concepts used in the compilation and preparation of all financial statements are:

1) *Accruals Concept*. This concept states that income earned and expenditure incurred should be accounted for in the period during which they occurred and not in a subsequent period. For example, if the accounting period ends on 31 December and an invoice is sent out on 23 December, that invoice should be included in the income figure for the period ended 31 December. This means that there will be a need for an increase in the figure owed to the business (the debtors). Similarly if work was done on 15 December (but no invoice received by 31 December), that cost should be reflected within the trading and profit and loss account, and the amount owed by the company (the creditors) increased. This is an outworking of the double-entry concept which you may have already studied.

2) *Consistency Concept*. This is a simpler concept that basically stresses that the business should apply the same accounting methods and policies from one period to the next. For example, if the business had used a straight-line depreciation method (see later) in Year 1, it should not switch to a reducing-balance method in Year 2 and then straight-line again in Year 3.

3) *Going Concern Concept*. Here the underlying assumption is that the business will continue to trade in the subsequent time period. Please note that while all accountants will prepare accounts on this basis, none will guarantee that the business will continue for another period.

4) *Materiality Concept*. Not all aspects of the business can be recorded. For example, a business employs 350,000 people, requires them do to a lot of writing and supplies them with pens. If only one in ten of these staff lose or break (*or borrow*) these pens then the company will have lost 3,500 pens, each worth, say, 50p. This is a cost of £1,750. Is it worth counting all the pens on 31 December to find out exactly how many are left? If each of the members was provided with a desktop or laptop computer does the question

of how many have been lost, broken or borrowed become more important? The value of the computers would be material whereas the value of the pens is not. Obviously the level of materiality differs from one business to another.

5) *Money Measurement Concept.* This requires that all the transactions have a definite and verifiable monetary value. If this is not the case then the transaction cannot be incorporated into the accounts. For example, if you work overtime and get paid, the cost will be reflected in the expenses of your employer. If, however, you received a day off in lieu of payment then the cost of your labour is effectively not reflected in the accounts.

6) *Prudence Concept.* This is perhaps the most important all of the concepts. This concept requires that a conservative approach is taken at all times. This means that profit should be accounted for only when made, whereas losses should be allowed for immediately. For example, if you have started a project and expect to make £1,500 profit when it is finished you cannot include the unmade profit in the current period results. On the other hand if you hear that one of your debtors is in financial difficulty you should immediately make a provision for the amount of the debt. When in doubt, understate profits and overstate losses.

7) *Separate Entity Concept.* The financial transactions of a business are to be treated separately from those of the owners. This causes some confusion in the minds of some sole traders and partnerships. This concept keeps the personal and business affairs separate for accounting purposes, although for legal purposes the businesses do not have a separate legal identity from the owners. Any debt owed by a non-corporate business is the liability of the owner.

There will be occasions when the application of one concept may seem to be at odds with another. For instance, under the accruals concept we should consider income earned but not received as an accrual. But under the prudence concept we should not count profit until it is made. How can we decide which concept to apply? In this case we could look to the materiality concept. If the invoice related to a small fraction of our income then it could, quite prudently, be included. If on the other hand it represented say 10% of our total income for the year it would be imprudent to implement the accruals concept in this case.

Because all of the concepts are open to differences in interpretation from one practitioner to another there will always be an element of uncertainty in all financial statements. In order to reduce the level of uncertainty the accountancy profession has developed a framework of rules and regulations known as:

>Statement of Standard Accounting Practice (SSAPs)

>and

>Financial Reporting Standards (FRSs)

These rules attempt to ensure that the interpretation of the concepts is as standardized as much as possible across the whole range of businesses. In terms of importance, the FRSs are slowly replacing the SSAPs, although many of the SSAPs still remain valid. It is not a requirement of this course that you know these rules but you should remember that they exist.

One of the outcomes of this framework of regulations is that all businesses produce the same set of financial statements on an annual basis. These are the trading and profit and loss account, the balance sheet and the statement of recognized gains and losses. Let us take a look at each one.

1. *The trading and profit and loss account*. This statement shows in a standard format how much profit the business has earned over a particular period. This is achieved by subtracting the cost of the goods sold and the expenses of the business from the income generated.

2. *The balance sheet*. This is a snapshot of the net worth of a business at the balance sheet date. The balance sheet is based on a standard basic formula which you must be comfortable with.

The ACCOUNTING EQUATION
ASSETS – LIABILITES = CAPITAL

4.1 Assets

The assets *owned* by the business are sub-divided into fixed assets and current assets.

Fixed assets

The fixed assets are generally considered to be those that have an element of permanence. They can be seen as the spine of a business and are those assets that will be used by the business more than once. The fixed assets are:

Property – land or land and buildings

Normally the place from which the business operates. If this is not owned but rented the value of the property will not be reflected in the balance sheet unless a long lease is in operation. A business can own a property and rent it out. The value of the property would appear in the balance sheet and the rental income in the profit and loss account.

Plant and machinery

Used in the business to produce goods, etc. This could, for example, be a lathe or a computer.

Fixtures and fittings

For example, tables and chairs in a restaurant.

Vehicles

Any vehicle owned by the business and used for business purposes. This would include company cars provided to staff.

A quick review of these fixed assets shows they have one thing in common – they are tangible, that is they can be seen and touched. This makes them reasonably easy to value, which is important as accurate valuation is one of the cornerstones of good accounting. A question. Does a value remain constant? If we think about our own assets for a moment we will realize that the answer is no. We will also realize that some assets increase in value (our houses) whereas others fall (our car, our computer, etc.). In the same way business assets either appreciate in value or depreciate. Assets that fall in value will eventually need to be replaced and by depreciating the asset on an annual basis the business is, technically, building up the resources to permit this. However, it is rare that theses resources are earmarked for a particular purpose.

How can we allow for these effects in the accounts. Back to the concepts and on to the SSAPS.

Look again at the fixed assets and you will see that, with the exception of property, all the assets are likely to fall in value as time goes by. Therefore it must be right and proper to reflect this reduction in the accounts. Image the chaos and scope for manipulation if this reduction were done on an ad hoc basis. In actual fact there are strict guidelines for the depreciation of assets which, by and large, will be done by two approved methods;

a) *straight-line depreciation* – Under this system the asset value is reduced by the same amount every year. The actual amount is determined by the lifetime of the asset. So that, if an asset cost £25,000 and has a lifetime of five years, then the depreciation charge will be 25,000/5,000 = £5,000 per annum. The value of the asset would reduce in the balance sheet as follows:

	Yr 1	Yr 2	Yr 3	Yr 4	Yr 5
Cost	25,000	25,000	25,000	25,000	25,000
Dep	5,000	10,000	15,000	20,000	25,000
¹WDV	20,000	15,000	10,000	5,000	nil

At the end of the fifth year the asset would appear as of no value even if it was still being used.

b) *Reducing-balance depreciation* – Some assets lose the majority of their value in the early years and therefore less later on. This rate of depreciation depends on the asset and a typical profile would be:

	Yr 1	Yr 2	Yr 3	Yr 4	Yr 5
Cost	25,000	25,000	25,000	25,000	25,000
Dep	12,000	18,000	21,000	23,000	25,000
WDV	13,000	7,000	4,000	2,000	nil

¹ Written-down value

Every year the depreciation charge will be deducted from the profit and loss account as an expense (this reduces both the profit and the tax). However, depreciation is a notional concept and no funds leave the business. Note that in examples (a) and (b) the total depreciation is the same but in (b) the profit shown would be £7,000 less (because the depreciation charge is 12,000-5,000 more). Once a business has started to depreciate an asset by any method then it must stick with that method (consistency).

As we leave depreciation it is worth mentioning that property is not subject to an annual change in value within the accounts. Property is normally shown at cost. On occasion it is necessary to reflect the change in value (especially after, say, 10-15 years). This is accomplished by a revaluation by approved valuers. This has the effect of strengthening the overall balance sheet and lenders should always be wary of a large revaluation reserve in the accounts because this might be hiding real problems.

Properties do not always appreciate and several (well-known) banks in the late 1980s and early 1990s had to make large provisions for potential bad debts due to overestimations of value and subsequent overgenerous lending.

Intangible fixed assets

A further group of fixed assets exists known as intangible fixed assets. These are assets that cannot be touched or seen. This makes them very difficult to value and we will not consider this aspect. For the sake of completeness we will, however, mention the most common – *goodwill*.

Goodwill is created within a business as its reputation grows, and disappears if that reputation is lost. If a business is taken over the purchaser will have to pay an amount to reflect the benefit obtained from this goodwill. An example would be Marks and Spencer plc. Any purchaser of the company would have to pay not only the value of the net assets of the company but also something (in the case of M&S a very big something!!) for the reputation. The main consideration with goodwill is that M&S cannot include the value of the goodwill in its balance sheet. It can be included only in the accounts of the buyer. This is further complicated by the fact that this value must be written off so that the value in the balance sheet reduces to zero over a few years.

There are a few other intangible fixed figure assets such as research and development, trademarks and brands, but again these are beyond the scope of this text.

Current assets

The second group of assets recorded within the balance sheet are the current assets. These have no long-term existence within the business and are usable only once. We could consider them to be the lifeblood of the business. They are:

Cash
Either in the tills and cash boxes of the business or in the current account of the business.

Once you have spent a fiver you cannot reuse it. You must get another one. Obviously very easy to value.

Stock

Not all businesses have stock. For example, an Internet service provider sells access to the Internet – can such access be stock? Other businesses have large amounts of stock – supermarkets are a good example. Some businesses, especially manufacturers, have three types of stock. This occurs if a business purchases an item (say a block of wood), carves it and sells the finished carving.

This business (normally a manufacturing company) will have:

- raw materials;
- work in progress;
- finished goods.

The danger with stock is that it can become unsaleable. In this case its value falls to nil and this in turns reduces profits. Overall the valuation of stock can be highly problematical. Assume you buy 200 items of identical stock and you sell 180. What is the value of the remaining 20?

a) Is it the value of the last 20 bought, i.e. you sold in the order you bought?

b) Is it the value of the first 20 you bought?

c) Is it the average value of all 200 which is applied to the remaining 20?

This apparently pointless scenario caused much confusion in the past. Some businesses chose method (a) this is called **First In First Out** (*FIFO*). Others chose method (b) **Last In First Out** (*LIFO*), and scenario (c) is called **Average Cost** (*AVCO*). The effect of choosing a different stock valuation method was to increase or decrease the level of profit in the business by adjusting the value of the stock .This occurs because gross profit is calculated as:

Sales – Cost of goods sold, where cost of goods sold is

(Opening stock plus purchases) less closing stock.

If we look at the scenario above there would be no problem if the cost of the stock was the same throughout the accounting period. If, however, the first 100 units were purchased at £10 per unit and the last 100 at £12 per unit we would have three different final stock valuations under the three different bases:

FIFO stock remaining is the last 20 bought at £12 each   Stock = 240

LIFO stock remaining is the first 20 bought at £10 each   Stock = 200

AVCO stock remaining is valued at the average of £11 each   Stock = 220

If we had sold all 180 at £20 each, our gross profit under each method would have been

Table 4.1

	FIFO		LIFO		AVCO
Sales	3,600		3,600		3,600
Opening stock	0		0		0
Purchases	2,200		2,200		2,200
Closing stock	*240*		*200*		*230*
Cost of goods sold		1,960		2,000		1,970
Gross profit		**1,640**		**1,600**		**1,630**

Thus, in this scenario, using the LIFO method has shown less gross profit (and thus less net profit). Is this a real difference or a difference arising from the accounting treatment of the stock? Obviously the latter. Why might a business want to show less profit? Well, taxes are based on profits and so if a lower profit is made (shown) then a lower tax charge will be levied. Similarly a business whose profits are lower than might be acceptable to shareholders or lenders could increase profits by adjusting the stock valuation method.

Eventually the Accounting Standards Board issued a SSAP which set limits on the stock valuation methods based on the concepts of prudence and consistency. This SSAP together with the restrictions imposed by the Companies Act 1985 have meant that stock should now be valued either by the FIFO method or AVCO. Both of these methods of valuation is subject to the overriding consideration that stock valuation should be "at the lower of cost (FIFO or AVCO) and net realizable value". Net realizable value is used to cover the situation of obsolescence. For example, 30,000 386-computer chips bought two years ago for 50p per chip are now worthless – their net realizable value is zero. The only prudent method of accounting for their value in the balance sheet is to record it as zero regardless of the original cost.

Debtors

These are those customers who owe you money. That is, they have yet to pay for the goods or services received from you. Most businesses have debtors although some do not. Your local chip shop will have no debtors (but they will have stock) whereas your local garage may have some debtors. Obviously it would be better if everybody paid you as soon as you supplied them, but many businesses extend credit to their customers to encourage those customers to stay with them. The major concern relating to debtors is "are you going to be paid?". In the normal course of events the answer would be yes . However, there will be occasions when the debtor cannot (or will not) pay. This might be due to his own financial problems or because there is a dispute over the quality of the goods or over the level of the outstanding debt. Is this debt still an asset? If we believe the debt will be repaid, fine – if however, we have doubts, we should (prudence) reduce the level of debtors and make a provision for the doubtful debt in the profit and loss account. Unfortunately there is no hard-

and-fast rule about what constitutes a doubtful debt. Certainly if a debtor has been refusing to pay an amount owed for six months, the chances of you being paid are low. But six weeks? Eight weeks? In practice a lender will consider the credit given period (see Chapter 5) to try to spot any problems. Increasingly, larger customers are asked for an aged list of debtors. This report, compiled by management, splits the debtors into time periods:

Business A

Aged list of debtors

less than 1 month	1-3 months	3-6 months	more than 6 months	Total
100,000	50,000	30,000	10,000	190,000

this is a great deal better than

Business B

less than 1 month	1-3 months	3-6 months	more than 6 months	Total
10,000	10,000	50,000	120,000	190,000

4.2　Liabilities

The liabilities are the amounts *owed* by the business. These are again split into current and long-term liabilities. Long-term liabilities are those due for repayment outside the current accounting period, i.e. repayment is more than twelve months away. They normally consist of loans used to purchase fixed assets and may or may not be secured on those assets. Generally speaking the lenders are receiving a fixed rate of interest on the debt and know the date of repayment of the loan.

Liabilities due for repayment within the accounting period are called current liabilities and ordinarily consist of:

Overdraft

This is monies owed to a banker on current account.

It is generally used by businesses as a trading facility to allow for the mismatch in time periods between goods bought and paid for, and goods sold and paid for. It is a vital part of most businesses within the UK and provides a bedrock of income to the lender.

Trade creditors

These are the suppliers who have not yet been paid. The granting of credit is a common business tactic as, it can be argued, it encourages buying. From one point of view the longer these remain unpaid the better. But remember that one man's creditor is the other man's debtor and the creditor will be seeking repayment. From the lender's point of view an increasing level of creditors is often a bad sign and may be accompanied by an increasing demand for an overdraft. If the bank increases the overdraft by £100,000 and the creditors go down by £100,000 who has benefitted? Certainly not the bank.

It is becoming common also to request an aged list of creditors from borrowing customers.

Tax

This is the amount owed to the Inland Revenue and is determined by the level of profits the business has made.

For sole traders the profit is taxed as income tax and for partnerships each partner's share of the profits is also treated as income and taxed accordingly. For corporate bodies the government levies corporation tax. Both income tax and corporation tax are staggered so that the greater the income the greater the tax.

Tax is a *preferential creditor*. This means that in the event of business failure the tax due gets paid before other debts.

Hire purchase

As an alternative to purchasing an expensive asset (which could involve a large capital outlay) the business can hire the asset from a third party. In exchange for not using the asset the third party receives regular payments from the business (lessor) for a fixed period of time. The agreement also obliges the lessor to purchase the asset at the end of the hire period.

Dividends

These are the share of the profits owed to, but not yet paid to, the company's shareholders. Obviously this type of liability does not exist in sole traders and partnerships.

Capital

This is the amount of the owner's money in the business. Remember the accounting equation?

$$\text{Assets} - \text{Liabilities} = \text{Capital}$$

This is also looked at in another way.

$$\text{Net worth} = \text{Capital}$$

The correct phraseology to use is:

The net worth of the business is financed by the capital.

The capital is the total of the original funds put into the business plus any reserves. Reserves, by and large, are created when a business makes a profit of, say, £10,000 but pays out only £5,000 to the owners. This creates a reserve of £5,000. This still belongs to the owners but is being kept in the business to allow the business to grow.

We know by now that things cannot be that simple and straightforward. Indeed there are three ways of expressing the capital, and the correct format depends upon whether the business is a sole trader, a partnership or a company.

If the business is a sole trader the capital section looks like this:

Capital	10,000
Profits	10,000
Less drawings	5,000
	15,000

A partnership is a little more complicated and it is highly unlikely that you will be asked to deal with a partnership situation in the exam, but partnership accounts consist of a capital account and a current account. At its simplest the capital account reflects the original capital and the current account represents the share of the profits less drawings. It is for each partner to decide how much, or how little, he draws in any year.

A company's capital is more straightforward. It comprises shares and reserves. The shares are normally *ordinary shares*, which carry voting rights and an entitlement to a share of the profits, and occasionally *preference shares*. These shares do not give a vote but receive a fixed dividend payment which must be paid before ordinary shareholders get anything.

As mentioned earlier, reserves are built up by leaving some of the earnings in the business each year as opposed to paying them all to the owners. Reserves can also come about from *accounting adjustments* such as revaluing a property and creating a revaluation reserve. Simply put, if a property bought for £50,000 in 1983 is now worth £ 500,000 then the balance sheet would be amended. The value of the fixed assets would go up by £450,000 and the financed-by section would also be increased by £450,000 by way of a revaluation reserve.

Case study: Bloggs Car Services

Let us put all this together.

Joe Bloggs wins £50,000 on the lottery and decides to start up a small business servicing cars. He finds a suitable building and agrees to rent it. He purchases some essential tools and equipment for £15,000 and puts the rest of the money into the bank account Bloggs Car Services.

The opening balance sheet would reflect this:

$$\text{Assets less Liabilities} = \text{Capital}$$

Table 4.2: Balance sheet for Bloggs Car Services as at 1 January 1999

Fixed assets			
Tangible	Equipment	15,000	(a)
Intangible		NIL	(b)
Total Fixed Assets		15,000	(c) = a+ b
Current assets			
Bank account	35,000 (d)		
Stock	nil (e)		
Debtors	nil (f)		
Total current assets		35,000 (g)	g = d +e + f
Current Liabilities			
Overdraft nil			
Creditors nil			
Hire purchase nil			
Tax nil			
Dividends nil			
Total current liabilities		nil (h)	
Current assets – Current liabilities		35,000	(i) = g – h
Total Net Assets		50000	(k) = c + i
Financed by			
Capital		50000	(l)

Please note

1) It is not normal to list assets or liabilities whose value is nil.

2) Figure (i) **This is a figure of major importance. It is called the working capital and is used in calculating several major ratios. We will refer to it repeatedly.**

3) k must always equal l. This is a balance sheet so assets minus liabilities equals capital.

After twelve months trading Joe needs to produce a new set of statements to show how his business has performed.

Table 4.3: The Trading and Profit and Loss account for Bloggs Car Services for the 12 months to 31 December 1999

Sales		60,225	
Opening stock	nil		
Purchases	5000		
	5000		
less closing stock	1,000	4,000	(this is the cost of goods sold)
Gross Profit		**56,225**	
Less expenses			
Wages	10,400		(for his employee £200 p.w.)
Insurance	200		
Advertising	200		
Depreciation	5,000		(suggests 3-year life of assets)
Heat/light	1,300		
Rent and rates	300	17,400	
Net Profit		**38,825**	

His balance sheet will now look something like this:

Table 4.4: Balance sheet for Bloggs Car Services as at 31 December 1999

Fixed assets

Tangible	Equipment at cost		15,000	
	less depreciation		<u>5,000</u>	<u>10,000</u>
Total Fixed Assets				10,000
Current assets				
Bank account		58,825		
Stock		1,000*		
Debtors		1,500		
Total current assets			61,325	
Current liabilities				
	Creditors	2,500		
Total current liabilities			2,500	
Current assets – Current liabilities				58,825
Total Net Assets				68,825
Financed by				
Capital				50,000
Profit		38,825		
Less drawings		<u>20,000</u>		<u>18,825</u>
				68,825

* Note that this is the same as the closing stock figure in the profit and loss account. It will become the opening figure for the profit and loss account for the year to 31.12.2000.

This is a good balance sheet.

- there is a lot of cash
- there are very few debtors
- Joe is leaving cash in the business.

The balance sheet could just as easily look like this:

Table 4.5: Balance sheet for Bloggs Car Services as at 31 December 1999

Fixed assets				
Tangible	Equipment at cost		15,000	
	less depreciation		5,000	10,000
Total fixed assets				10,000
Current assets				
Bank account		26,825		
Stock		1,000		
Debtors		1,500		
Total current assets			29,325	
Current liabilities				
	Creditors	2,500		
Total current liabilities			2,500	
Current assets – Current liabilities				26,825
Total Net Assets				36,825
Financed by				
Capital				50,000
Profit		38,825		
Less drawings		52,000		(13,175)
				36,825

This is not as good. It is still not bad but by paying himself £1,000 p.w. Joe is paying more than the business can afford. This can obviously not continue for many years.

To continue. On 1 January Joe takes in a partner. This partner, Fred, has no cash but brings in a building which he transfers into their joint names. This enables Joe to hire two new mechanics and triple his turnover. The business buys another £15,000 of tools. The profit and loss account could look something like this.

Table 4.6: The Trading and Profit and Loss account for Bloggs Car Services for the 12 months to 31 December 2000

Sales		201,225
Opening stock	1,000 =	last year's closing stock
Purchases	<u>25,000</u>	
	26,000	
less closing stock	<u>5,000</u>	<u>21,000</u>
Gross Profit		**180,225**
Less expenses		
Wages	31,200	
Insurance	600	a bigger premises
Advertising	200	
Depreciation	10,000	5,000 for two years
Heat/light	2,500	
Rates	<u>300</u>	<u>44,800</u>
Net Profit		**135,425**

The balance sheet will now look something like this:

Table 4.7: Balance sheet for Bloggs Car Services as at 31 December 2000

Fixed assets			
Building	At valuation		30,000
Tangible	Equipment at cost	30,000	
	less depreciation	<u>15,000</u>*	<u>15,000</u>
Total fixed assets			45,000
Current assets			
Bank account	83,750		
Stock	5,000		
Debtors	4,000		
Total current assets		92,750	
Current liabilities			
	Creditors	7,500	
Total current liabilities		7,500	
Current assets – Current liabilities			85,250
Total Net Assets			130,250

Financed by

	Joe	Fred	
Capital account	50,000	30,000	
Current account	18,825	Nil	
Share profits	<u>67,713</u>	<u>67,712</u>	
	136,538	97,712	
Less drawings	52,000	52,000	
	84,538	45,712	130,250

* 5,000 from 1999 and 10,000 from 2,000.

Another stunningly good year and as bankers we would be dying to lend to this partnership.

To continue. On 1 January the partners take the advice of their accountants and solicitors and decide to become a limited company. They convert all their reserves into shares and the financed-by section of the balance sheet, on the 1 January 2001 becomes:

Ordinary Share capital £1 each   Authorized 250,000

Issued   130,250   130,250

This does not affect the rest of the balance sheet which reflects the transfer of the assets and liabilities to the company as at 31 December 2000.

The first trading year for Bloggs Car Services Ltd. is detailed below:

Table 4.8: The Trading and Profit and Loss account for Bloggs Car Services Ltd for the 12 months to 31 December 1999

Sales		105,222	
Opening stock	5,000		
Purchases	35,000		
	40,000		
Less closing stock	25,000	15,000	
Gross Profit		**90,222**	
Less expenses			
Wages	61,200		
Insurance	700		
Advertising	500		
Depreciation	5,000		The assets bought off partnership were valued at 15,000
Heat/light	1,500		
Rates	800	69,700	
Net Profit before tax		**20,522**	
Tax		**7,222**	
Net Profit after tax		**13,300**	**EARNINGS**
Retained profits from last year		**00000**	
Proposed dividend		**3,300**	
Transfer to reserves		**10,000**	

Note that tax appears in the company accounts because the company, and not the shareholders, is responsible for the tax on the profits.

If there were any interest due – from loans or overdrafts – these would appear in the expenses section and would be deducted *before* tax. Interest is a tax-deductible expense.

Note also that the dividends are paid after tax. The tax liability is the shareholders'.

The split between retained profits and dividends is at the discretion of the directors subject to the shareholders approval at the Annual General Meeting. Hence the term *proposed dividend*. The balance sheet would look like this.

Table 4.9: Balance sheet for Bloggs Car Services Ltd as at 31 December 2001

Fixed asset			30,000
Tangible	Equipment at cost	15,000	
	less depreciation	5,000	10,000
Total Fixed Assets			40,000
Current assets			
Bank account	87,250		
Stock	25,000		
Debtors	25,000		
Total current assets		137,250	
Current liabilities			
Creditors	37,000		
Total current liabilities	37,000		
Current assets – Current liabilities			100,250
Total Net Assets			140,250
Financed by			
Share capital 130,250 shares @1		130,250	
Profit and loss account		10,000	
			140,250

Has this been a good first year for Bloggs Car Services Ltd.?

Well, the company has made a profit and kept most of it in the business. There is over £80,000 in the bank account. These are always good signs. On the down side, the sales are just over half of what they were for the partnership. This must surely be investigated. Other worrying signs are the big increase in closing stock and the massive increase in both debtors and creditors.

Before considering a specific lending proposition let us review what we have done so far. We have just spent over 5,000 words looking at the financial statements prepared by a business to record its performance over a period of twelve months.

These can be summarized as follows:

The *trading, and profit and loss account*: a report of the income and expenses of a business over a year.

The *balance sheet*: a snapshot of the assets and liabilities of business on a particular date.

In addition to these (which many mistakenly think of as *the accounts*) there are two other *primary financial statements*. These are the *statement of recognized gains and losses* – known affectionately as $SORG$ – and the *cash flow statement*.

SORG attempts to show the profit for the accounting period together with other movements in shareholder reserves. Study of SORG is not necessary within this module. There are currently, within accountancy circles, some concerns regarding the value and appropriateness of SORG.

Cash flow statement

The cash flow statement is, however, a tool whose use is seen as very valuable. It shows, in a tabular form, the total movements of cash within a business. The importance of a good cash flow within a business cannot be overstated. William Buffet, the US investment guru, makes a strong positive cash flow a prerequisite for investment.

The cash flow statement format

Net cash flow from operating activities	xxx
Returns on investments and servicing of finance	yyyy
Taxation – *this will normally be a negative figure*	zzzz
Investing activities – *often negative*	aaaa
Financing	bbbb
Increase in cash and cash equivalents	TTTT the sum of above

This statement is supported by four Notes of which we need consider only Note 1.

Note 1: Reconciliation of operating profit to net cash inflow from operating profit

	Source of information
Operating profit	From profit and loss account
Depreciation charge	From profit and loss account
Profits/Losses on sale of fixed assets	From profit and loss account
Change in stocks	From balance sheet
Change in debtors	From balance sheet
Change in creditors	From balance sheet
TOTAL	xxx Note that this is the starting figure in the cash flow statement

These changes refer to the difference between one balance sheet and the subsequent year's balance sheet, e.g.

	1998	1997
Debtors	12,000	10,000 an increase on debtors

The following rules need to be followed in constructing Note 1:

1. The operating profit may be a loss.

2. Depreciation is *added back* to operating profit because, while it is deducted as an expense, it does not leave the business. All other expenses (e.g. wages payments) actually leave the business.

3. If a loss is made on the sale of a fixed asset this loss is added back. A profit made on the sale of fixed assets is subtracted. The reasons for this spring from ramifications of depreciation that do not need to be considered.

4. The following rules apply for changes in stocks:

	Action
Increase in stock	Subtract
Decrease in stock	Add

5. The following rules apply for changes in debtors:

	Action
Increase in debtors	Subtract
Decrease in debtors	Add

6. The following rules apply for changes in creditors:

	Action
Increase In creditors	Subtract
Decrease in creditors	Add

In addition to the primary financial statements you should take care not to ignore the notes that often accompany them. These contain valuable qualitative information such as a breakdown of directors' shareholding, accounting policies and the auditor's statement. These items will not be shown for companies with smaller turnovers but are a legal requirement for larger ones. In such companies the report of the auditor is very important. Normally the auditor's report is phrased on the following lines:

> *In our opinion the accounts give a true and fair view of the state of affairs of the company at 31 December 1998 and the profit for the company for the fifty two weeks then ended and have been properly prepared in accordance with the Companies Act 1989.*

Any deviation from the above clean report would be a cause for serious concern.

4.3   Management accounts

The problem with all these statements is that by the time they become available to a potential lender they are out-of-date. This might be by only three months but can be as much as twelve. So how can we know what is happening *now*?

Every large business, and many smaller ones, now produces (for its own benefit) an internally generated set of *management accounts*. This process has been made substantially easier by various software packages. It is possible to purchase off-the-shelf bookkeeping and accounting packages inexpensively or, for more complex businesses, to tailor-make a package based on the industry-standard spreadsheet packages. The essence of all these programs is that the operator inputs all the day's business – sales, purchases, wages, etc. – and the program translates these details into the approved financial statement formats.

The value of this is immense. A business is able to see daily how it is performing, and to take action to correct problems or take advantage of opportunities.

From the lender's point of view the figures show an up-to-date picture. While this picture might not be completely accurate, it will be a far clearer picture than accounts that are six months old unless the management is trying to pull the wool over your eyes.

In addition to producing accounts, many businesses – often at the behest of their bankers – are producing forecast figures. These are a projected profit and loss account and balance sheet based on the last audited accounts and what the management of the business thinks (believes) will be achieved in the current trading year.

The best businesses not only produce forecasts of future performance, but also formulate the plans that will, they hope, assist in achieving them.

Budgets are a mechanism whereby the quality of the forecasts and the efficacy of the plans can be checked. The main budgets are:

Sales budget

Shows the expected sales on a month-by-month basis for the business as a whole or for different sections of the business. If you had 300 different products it would be important to know that, while sales overall were up, that sales of everything were up. Tesco management might see that sales are up 4%. This is good but what if this is based on a 150% increase in coffee sales and an 80% fall in tea sales? Can this be ignored or is some action indicated?

Cash flow

Cash flow is vital to a business. Even banks. Too much cash in tills is unproductive, as are large cash balances in bank accounts. So a business will want to plan for the most efficient level of liquid cash.

Stock

Somewhat linked to the sales budget. If tea is not selling do you want to keep high levels of tea in stock? If you are overstocked this is going to adversely affect your profits.

Expenses

A prime area for improving profitability is in the control of expenses. In some ways expenses are far easier to forecast than sales. Telephone costs will increase by a known amount. Thus if the level of calls remains constant then the cost this year will be x % greater than last year. If the first quarter's bill is in excess of this then the *number* of calls must have increased.

With expenses one important fact needs to be borne in mind. Is the expense *fixed* or *variable*? A fixed cost will not rise as production or sales rise and so should be very easy to budget. A variable cost will increase as sales increase. This means that the link between the level of sales and the expense needs to be established. This is a specialized area of accountancy which you will encounter in a few years time. Budgeting for variable costs can prove quite complex.

Cash flow forecast

Probably the most important budget produced is the *cash flow forecast*.

This enables a business and its banker to consider what level of cash will be in the business's current account and whether or not an overdraft will be required.

A standard cash flow consists of all income and expenditure items expected within the business and is shown below:

Table 4.10: Standard cash flow forecast

	Jan	Feb	March	April	May	June
Sales	20,000	20,000	20,000	20,000	20,000	20,000
Receipts						
Cash	5,000	5,000	5,000	5,000	5,000	5,000
Credit		15,000	15,000	15,000	15,000	15,000
Total	5,000	20,000	20,000	20,000	20,000	20,000

Expenditure

	Jan	Feb	March	April	May	June
Purchases	12,000	12,000	12,000	12,000	12,000	12000
Wages	3,000	3,000	3,000	3,000	3000	3,000
Power			1,000			1,000
Rent	500			500		
Rates		250			250	
Telephone		175			175	
Interest	-1,500			1,500		
Total	14,000	15,425	16,000	17,000	15,425	16,000
Opening bal.	-3,000	-12,000	-7,425	-3,425	-425	4,150
Net cash flow	-9,000	4,575	4,000	3,000	4,575	4,000
Close bal.	-12,000	-7,425	-3,425	-425	4,150	8,150

Let us consider the above cash flow without going into too much detail. Detailed study of cash flows will be undertaken in future modules, although we will construct one at the end of this chapter.

- All figures will be estimates.

- The forecast will normally be for a full twelve months' trading period.

- In January £20,000 of sales are made. However, only £5,000 of the sales are for cash with the remaining £15,000 made on credit. The length of credit will be different for different customers so in our example the full £15,000 is received in February. In reality perhaps only £8,000 will be received in February with the remainder not received until March. This *staggered* receipt of income will continue throughout the year. At the end of the year the amount of sales made on credit which has not been paid for will form the debtors of the business and will appear as an asset in the balance sheet.

- Notice that some of the expenses are monthly and some quarterly. The list of expenses shown is by no means exhaustive.

- The opening balance for January will be taken form the last balance sheet dated 31 December.

- The cash flow forecast shows that this business will require an overdraft for the first four months.

- Just as credit is given on sales it is probable that the company will be taking credit on its purchases and there will be a stagger caused by this. Indeed if the business *took* credit for only one month the need for an overdraft would seem to disappear.

The most important test for all budgets, including the cash flow forecast, is "how close do they match actual performance?"

At the end of January the management will look at the actual performance and if necessary take corrective action. Precision is not expected in budgets; there are far too many variables. However the actual figures should be in the ballpark of the projections. For example, an actual overdraft at the end of January of between £10,500 and £14,000 would be acceptable whereas an overdraft of £28,000 would be cause for serious concern.

Constructing cash flow forecasts

The example given above is perhaps a trifle unusual. Not in its format or the figures but purely because of its existence. The majority of smaller business customers do not produce cash flows or they produce inadequate or incomplete versions. The construction and/or correction of cash flow forecasts is an *essential* skill for all lenders so we had better work through an example.

Your customer Mr M. Parry approaches you with a business proposition. He has decided to become a self-employed computer analyst and has been awarded two contracts from major local companies. He says he will need to rent a service unit and purchase some essential equipment. He asks for a loan of £10,000 that he says will be sufficient to set him up.

You question Mr Parry and obtain the following financial information:

- *one contract is for £15,000 per year and will be paid in quarterly instalments in arrears;*

- *the second contract is for £25,000 and will be paid monthly in arrears, payment starting at the end of the second month of the contract;*

- *the rent for the unit is £6,000 per year payable every month;*

- *Mr Parry says he needs £1,500 per month drawings;*

- *the rent does not include power, rates or insurance which are estimated at £250 per quarter, £150 per quarter and £600 per year (payable in two instalments).*

Let us see how these facts translate into a cash flow.

- contract one will be paid in four instalments of £3,750;

- contract two will be paid in twelve instalments of £2,083.33;

- the rent is £500 per month. This will normally be paid in advance;

- as Mr Parry will need his living expenses the drawings will start in Month 1;

- power will be paid in arrears;

- rates and insurance are payable in advance;

It is these figures that we will put into the cash flow.

Table 4.11: Cash flow

	1	2	3	4	5	6
Turnover	3,333.33	3,333.33	3,333.33	3,333.33	3,333.33	3,333.33
Receipts						
Cash						
Contract one			3,750.00			3,750.00
Contract two		2,083.33	2,083.33	20,83.33	20,83.33	2,083.33
Total	0000	2,083.33	5,833.33	20,83.33	20,83.33	5,833.33
Expenditure						
Purchases						
Drawings	1,500	1,500	1,500	1,500	1,500	1,500
Power			250			250
Rent	500	500	500	500	500	500
Rates	150			150		
Telephone						
Insurance	300			300		
Interest						
Total	2,450	2,000	2,250	2,150	2,000	2,250
Opening bal.	0000	-2,450	-2,366.67	-1,216.66	-1,283.33	-1,200.00
Net cash flow	-2,450	83.33	3,583.33	-66.67	83.33	3,583.33
Close bal.	-2,450	-2,366.67	-1,216.66	-1,283.33	-1,200.00	2,383.33

Note: The most frequent failings with cash flows is arithmetical errors. So I have incorporated a miscast in the above table. Where is it?

Some points should by now be clear.

Some expenses seem to have been ignored. Why has Mr Parry not considered them?

It is unclear where Mr Parry gets his figure of £10,000. Or what he wants it for? Is it for working capital or for asset purchase? If for working capital then the cash flow does not support that level of need. If it is for asset purchase then the following questions need to be asked:

• What is the total cost of the assets being purchased?

- How capital will be introduced?

Research time. Adjust the above cash flow for a full year incorporating the following facts.

- *Mr Parry will put £5,000 of his own money in to open the account.*

- *The loan is to buy a van. It will cost £15,000 and Mr Parry will pay a £5,000 deposit in addition to the £5,000 used to open the account.*

- *The loan requested is a twelve-month personal loan costing £933.33 p.m.*

- *Purchases will be a minimal amount and invoiced directly to the customer.*

5

RATIO ANALYSIS

Having discussed financial statements we will now consider how we can analyse them in a meaningful and consistent manner. To start let us ensure that we are comfortable with the standard accounting pro-formas for limited companies. Let us consider a small limited company.

5.1   Alfa Ltd – Standard Accounting Pro-formas

Table 5.1: Trading and Profit and Loss Account for the twelve months ended 5 April 1999

		Note
Sales	**225,900**	1
Cost of sales	(150,000)	2
Gross Profit	**75,900**	3
Distribution costs		4
Administration cost	47,000	5
NPBT&I	**28,900**	6
Interest payable	5,000	7
Taxation	3,000	8
NPAT&I	**20,900**	9
Dividends	10,900	10
Retained profit carried forward	**10,000**	11

Notes

1   Often called turnover.

2   May be shown as opening stock + purchases – closing stock.

3   The starting point for a successful business. If you cannot sell something for more than it cost you to make or buy, you are in trouble. The ratio sales/cost of sales is called the mark up. The larger the mark up the larger the gross profit. *Think about it.*

4 Some businesses have no distribution costs. Others incorporate them into the administration costs. Those businesses that show it separately do so because it forms a major cost element.

5 These include rent, wages, etc.

6 Net profit before tax and interest.

7 This is payable on loans and overdrafts.

8 Paid to the government. Generally the amount paid is not obviously related to the profit figure. This is because of timing differences and other factors.

9 Net profit after tax and interest, often called the earnings. This is the amount available to give to the shareholders as a dividend.

10 As previously discussed there is no rule of what has to be paid out to shareholders.

11 This is the amount retained from the earnings to strengthen the capital base of the company. Note this is the same figure as Figure 10 in the balance sheet below.

Table 5.2: Balance Sheet as at 5 April 1999

Fixed Assets					Note
Freehold premises			45,000		1
Plant and machinery	Cost	20,000			
	Depreciation	5,000	15,000		2
Motor vehicles	Cost	12,000			
	Depreciation	2,000	10,000	70,000	
Current Assets					
Stock		21,000			3
Debtors		20,000			4
Bank		2,500	43,500		5
Current Liabilities					
Creditors		23,500	23,500		6
NET CURRENT ASSETS				20,000	7
Long-term liabilities					
Loan		(15,000)	(15,000)		8

TOTAL NET ASSETS		75,000	
Financed by			
50,000 £1 ordinary shares	50,000		9
Retained profit	15,000		
Profit for the year	10,000		10
		75,000	

Notes

1. Generally speaking freehold property is not depreciated. This is because properly maintained properties appreciate in value; often the financed-by section reflects this. The existence of a revaluation reserve shows that the company has increased the value of its property in the balance sheet.

2. Depreciation is deducted from the asset cost. The balance sheet depreciation is not the same as the figure in the profit and loss account. It is, rather, the accumulation of the depreciation charged in all previous years.

3. Some companies – specifically manufacturing companies – split their stock into:

   - raw materials;
   - work in progress;
   - finished goods.

4. Often debtors are split into trade and other debtors.

5. The bank account appears as creditor if overdrawn.

6. Creditors can be further split into trade and other creditors.

7. This is also called working capital.

8. This loan may well be owed to a financial institution. In a public limited company there may be the following legend:

   6% Debenture 2009

   This means that the loan will pay 6 % interest and be repaid by the company in 2009. The term *debenture* indicates that the loan is secured and, in the event of the company being wound up, the lenders will benefit from the sale proceeds of the security.

9. The share capital is always a function of the number of shares and the nominal value. Thus, if the 50,000 shares were 50p nominal (as opposed to a £1), the capital figure in the balance sheet would be £25,000. Note that it is only the issued shares that form the capital.

10. This figure comes from the profit and loss account for the year ended 5 April.

The above figures in isolation tell us that the company is making a profit and has money in the bank, but very little else. And the figures for Alfa Ltd. are very simple. As a company gets larger the figures get more complicated and it becomes more difficult to discern anything meaningful. As lenders we use *ratio analysis* as the framework upon which we based many business-lending decisions. It is the process by which the lender utilizes the information supplied by the business (usually compiled and approved by auditors) to gain an impression of the creditworthiness, or otherwise, of the business. Ratios are useful because they summarize data in a user-friendly format so that the performance of a company in a current year can be compared with performance in previous years. This comparison, and the trends it reveals, is used to make a judgement about future performance. However, as advertisements for investments are obliged to point out,

> *past performance is no guarantee of future returns.*

so care needs to be exercised when considering any past performance. But what else does a potential lender have as guide? The use of ratios allows trends, or patterns, to be considered rather than individual items of data. It is generally accepted that figures covering three years, or four performances, are far more useful than two. You will recall from your studies in mathematics that plotting a graph from two readings can be very misleading. The consensus opinion is that figures over a longer period than four years lose some relevance due to their age. Having said this, many public limited companies will use five-year performance figures when showing positive trends in earnings, dividend and share-price growth.

Before proceeding to a more detailed discussion of the various ratios there are a few points that need to be made and that should always be considered when analysing business performance.

1) Accounts are generally between six and nine months old when received by a lender and at best provide a snapshot of the business *as at* the accounting date. In many instances this drawback is overcome by using management accounts prepared in house by the business. These have the advantage of being far more up to date but suffer from the lack of independent auditing.

2) Accounts are prepared to meet the needs of a number of different users. From your previous studies you should be aware that these include the shareholders, tax authorities and creditors. The best that can be said is that accounts please all of the people some of the time, some of the people all of the time but not all of the people all of the time.[1]

   One of the major disadvantages of management accounts is that they may have been prepared to highlight certain areas (e.g. profitability) that are of particular importance to the reader. A prudent lender will always consider management accounts with a greater degree of skepticism than audited accounts. It is not unheard of for the management accounts for 12 months to be quite different from the audited accounts for the same period.

3) Although all the accounts are prepared under agreed rules and frameworks [2] it is necessary to be aware of the limitations imposed by these rules and that different treatments of

---

[1] To paraphrase Abraham Lincoln.
[2] SSAPs (Statement of Standard Accounting Practice) and FRS (Financial Reporting Standards).

such things as asset valuation and depreciation will on occasions lead to some ambiguity.

4) The ratios and the trends determined from comparing year 199x with 199y and 199z are important in their own right. However they should never be relied upon in isolation and should always be supplemented by comparison with the ratios and trends from other companies in the same business sector. This is called inter-firm comparison (as opposed to intra-firm comparison) and enables a business to be assessed in broader terms. For example, if company A has seen sales increase by 3% more than inflation[3] per year for the last five years, this may seem a good sign. If, however, the average sales growth for similar companies in the same field is 12% the management needs to be questioned.

5) Accounts are prepared on a historic cost account basis that ignores the effect of inflation on prices and asset values. For many years the continued use of this basis of accounting has been the subject of major debate in financial circles. The main problem with historic cost accounting is that it assumes that the value of money remains stable all the time. This is not historically accurate. While inflation in the UK (and much of the rest of the industrialized world) is low, there have been prolonged periods when inflation has been in double figures. If inflation is 10% for seven years the purchasing power of £100 falls to approximately £48. Conversely the value of a fixed asset (such as a building) rises from £100 to £195. These two sides of the inflationary coin obviously mean that debtors of £15,000 in 1994 are different from debtors of £15,000 in 1999. The question that arises – and causes most of the problems within *inflation accounting* – is what would be the 1999 equivalent of £15,000 worth of 1994 debtors?

The primary arguments for compiling accounts on the alternative current cost accounting basis are:

a) Current cost accounting more fairly reflects the true value of assets held within a business for any significant length of time.

b) Current cost accounting also enables profits that have been artificially enhanced by inflationary effects to be correctly reported in real terms.

The major counter arguments are practical in nature rather than theoretical.

a) What measurement of inflation should be used?

b) Is this measure equally valid for all businesses?

c) Is the chosen inflation measurement equally applicable to all aspects of the business? For example, wage rate inflation may have very little relation to property price inflation or the increase in the costs of raw materials.

d) Are the subsequently produced figures worth the extra effort of producing them? In 1986 the *Byatt Report*[4] stated:

the measurement errors involved in estimating the cost of using resources in current prices pales into significance compared with those involved in ignoring the effect of

[3] Sales increases that are less than the rate of inflation are not real improvements.
[4] *Accounting for Economic Costs and Changing Prices.* HM Treasury 1986.

changing prices, in spite of the extra degree of judgement involved.

Although this suggests strongly that accounts should be adjusted to reflect inflationary effects, in practice very few businesses do so. As yet the debate continues and I strongly suspect that there will not be a major move towards the compulsory or popular use of current cost accounting in the short term.[5]

However, having considered the failings of the accounting statements available to us what else is there to base our lending considerations on? Nothing. Therefore using ratios and ratio analysis to discern trends is "the only game in town".

What is a ratio?

a quantitative relationship between two numbers.

Suppose in 1996 a small family car cost £7,500 and a large family car cost £15,000. Thus the ratio of the prices is 15000/7500 = 2 to 1. This says that the large car is twice the price of a small car.

In 1999 the prices were 8995 and 17250 respectively. The ratio is now 17250/8995 = 1.92 to 1. Thus we can say that the relationship between the two prices has altered. This could be expressed in one of two ways:

● the price of large family cars has come down in relation to small cars;

● the price of small cars has increased in relation to large cars.

Whichever way we express it, however, the large car is better value, in relation to the small car, in 1999 than it was in 1996.

Ratio analysis is broken down into five broad groupings. Not everybody will be interested in all five and some users will be concerned only with one of the groups. In practice most ratio users will look at all the ratios but place greater importance on a few.

The five main groups follow.

5.2   Capital structure

Fixed assets/net worth: this ratio shows the proportion of long-term assets provided by the shareholders' funds. Any shortfall must obviously be provided by borrowing. The existence of borrowing is not, in and of itself, a problem, provided that the term of the borrowing is less than the lifetime of the asset(s) and that the level of borrowing is serviceable.

Net worth/total assets: this ratio measures the owner's stake within the business. Generally the higher this ratio the more financially secure is the business. This ratio is linked to the level of company *gearing*, which we will discuss shortly.

Interest cover: is a measurement of how readily the business can cover the costs of fixed interest debt.

---

[5] For which students should be extremely grateful.

The formula is:

$$\frac{\text{Profit before interest and tax}}{\text{Interest payable}}$$

These debts are usually long-term and the costs a continuing drain on the business. A good level of cover is, therefore, essential and a significant fall in cover would be a cause for concern for lenders and investors, both existing and potential.

Gearing

Gearing is one of the most important ratios and often the first a prospective lender will calculate. It shows how the business is being financed. In a business with no borrowing all the funds are provided by the owners and gearing is zero. This obviously means that no lenders are at risk. It also means that no lenders are earning interest. If all businesses had zero gearing financial institutions would be in trouble. On the other hand the owners could be providing very little[6] capital and the creditors providing the bulk of the financing. While this obviously means that a lot of interest due is going to be generated, it also means that a lot of profit has to be generated to pay the interest. This problem is exacerbated in times of rising interest rates unless the bulk of the debt is fixed interest. The problem of high gearing is even more serious with limited companies because the shareholders have nothing to lose (other than the investment value of their shares) if the company were to fail. The cost of failure would be borne by the creditors.

Obviously some balance needs to be struck between no lending, no risk and no interest and big lending, lots of interest and lots of risk.

The formula for gearing is:

$$\frac{\text{Long-term debt}}{\text{Shareholders funds} + \text{Long-term debt}}$$

A currently popular third alternative is **net gearing**:

$$\frac{\text{Total debt} - \text{Cash}}{\text{Shareholders' funds}}$$

Total debt is long-term debt plus overdrafts plus hire purchase and leasing commitments. This is a more stringent test and widely used in financial institutions.

It is obviously vitally important that we are consistent in our usage. If we are, we should not encounter any problems. If we are not, then our calculations are worthless.

Of course we need to know what the magic figures are. As a general rule of thumb many would say:

---

[6] Every business must have some capital.

less than 50% good, more than 50 % bad

but different businesses have different acceptable gearing limits. For example, it is not unusual for a firm of builders to have gearing in excess of 100%, whereas gearing of 40% in a hairdressing business would be a cause for concern. Different financial institutions also enforce different ground rules and we should be aware of these.

5.3   Asset utilization

Sales/Fixed assets

This ratio measures the efficiency of utilization of fixed assets. Generally the higher the better, but do not forget to view on an inter-firm basis as well as intra-firm.

$$\textbf{Stock turnover period} \qquad \frac{\text{Average stock}^7}{\text{Cost of sales}} \quad \times 365$$

This ratio is correctly considered by many to be very important because it measures how frequently the stock is turned over (sold). Again there is no hard-and-fast rule as to what is good or acceptable. For example, a florist would want to be turning over its stock far more quickly than a car retailer. Obviously this figure benefits greatly from inter-firm comparisons. An asset turnover period of 12 days for a car dealer would be considered good but in the florists would be a disaster. But is it useful to compare a car dealers with a florists?

Asset turnover is very useful in aiding in the identification of stock that remains unsold for a longer than expected period. One of the reasons for this may be that the stock is obsolete (e.g. 386 computer chips). The implication of obsolete stock is that the company will be unable to sell the stock at the projected prices (if at all), and this will obviously impact on the profits of the company. Stock that is obsolete must be written off. This means that the value of the obsolete stock must be deducted from the profit for the trading period. This might reduce the level of profit carried forward to the balance in that year. A worst case scenario would be for the write-off to be larger than the profit. This would reduce the retained profit in the business. There have been several cases where the level of obsolescence has been so high that the business has been unable to withstand the write-off.

$$\textbf{Debtor collection period} \qquad \frac{\text{Average trade debtors}}{\text{Credit sales}} \quad \times 365$$
$$\text{(Credit given)}$$

$$\textbf{Creditor payment period} \qquad \frac{\text{Average trade creditors}}{\text{Credit purchases}} \quad \times 365$$
$$\text{(Credit taken)}$$

If you are not given the credit sales or credit purchases you can use the sales and purchase figures respectively. The effect of using these second figures will understate the turnover period, thus making it look more efficient.

[7]   (Opening stock +closing stock)/2.

Both these figures express, in terms of days, the time taken to collect the debts of the business or to pay the creditors. These figures are two sides of the same coin. The quicker a business can collect the money owed to it the better. It gets no interest on this money[8], therefore uncollected debts are effectively a free source of finance to the debtor. Conversely, the longer it takes a business to pay the money it owes the better. Here it benefits from the free source of finance.

Every business would like its debtors to pay it within a month and its creditors to allow it to pay after three months. There will always be a discrepancy between the two and usually a bank overdraft takes up the slack.

Just as stock can become obsolete so can debtors. Some debtors will never pay. If a business comes to realize that a debt might not be repaid – the debt is outstanding beyond, say, six months[9], then a provision for the bad debt will be made in the profit and loss account, thus reducing the profit. If the debt eventually gets paid the provision can get reversed. If the debt is not going to be repaid – the debtor is insolvent – then the debt is written off, again through the profit and loss account.

> *Research time: get the accounts of your employer and look at the level of provisions they are making.*

The main use of these ratios is to assess how efficiently a business is managing its cash and cash-equivalent resources. For example, an increase in the debtors' collection period figure may indicate a change in policy to increase sales, which is acceptable (within limits) or might show a new found laxity in collecting debts (change of staff?). It may also indicate that some debtors are not paying because they are unable to. A well-run business will, as previously mentioned, maintain an aged list of debtors to spot this.

Similarly an increase in the credit payment period figure might reflect that better terms have been negotiated with (or offered) by suppliers because of an increased purchase from them or, more sinisterly, might be a deliberate ploy because the business cannot really afford to pay. Remember that one man's creditor is another mans debtor and eventually the creditor will push for payment. This is when the bank account comes under pressure (or a request to increase the overdraft facility is received) as the business attempts to satisfy the creditor using bank funds.

5.4 Profitability

To survive any business must be profitable and continue to be profitable on a regular and frequent basis. While a business can survive a few years of low profitability or losses, if these continue for long time the business either ends up in liquidation or as a subsidiary of another business. Often loss-making businesses are taken over because the buyer wishes to acquire some portion of the target business – perhaps its name or a product or supply/distribution channels. In these cases the buyer will keep what is wanted and sell the rest. This process is known as *asset stripping*.

---

[8]   New legislation is now in force to allow interest to be charged but its effectiveness has yet to be seen.
[9]   Again this varies from business to business.

The key ratios, which are all expressed as percentages, are:

Gross profit margin	=	Gross profit/Sales
Net profit margin	=	Net profit before interest and tax/Sales
Operating margin	=	Overheads/Sales

Note that all these margins use the sales figures as a denominator. The practical effect of this is that a comparison can be made with a business with £20,000 net profit and a business with £ 2,000,000 net profit.

For example:

Net profit	**Sales**	**NPM**		
Company A	20,000	180,000	$\dfrac{20000}{180,000}$	11.11%
Company B	2,000,000	25,000,000	$\dfrac{2,000,000}{25,000,000}$	8.00%

Which of the two companies is performing best for its owners? The tendency would initially be to say that 11% is better than 8% and, all other things being equal, this could be true. However, no one ratio, looked at in isolation, can tell us a great deal about the business or its performance. None of the above profitability ratios takes into consideration the level of capital invested in the business by the owners. If both of the businesses have capital of £1,000,000 then 11% is better than 8%. But what if Company A has twice the level of capital of Company B?

An important ratio that addresses this problem is the *return on capital employed*. This ratio is normally expressed as:

$$\frac{\text{Profit before interest and tax}}{\text{Capital and reserves} + \text{Long-term liabilities}}$$

An acceptable variation on this, which looks at return on a company's net assets, is:

$$\frac{\text{Profit after tax}}{\text{Capital and reserves}}$$

You should note that, as we are now considering the net assets, we must consider only the amount of profit available to the owners. Therefore, as the owners receive a return only after interest to creditors and tax has been paid, these costs need to be deducted from the profit before calculating the return on capital employed.

When considering what constitutes an acceptable ROCE we are again faced with the problem of "different strokes for different folks". Similarly consistency year on year is important, and is the preferred variant of various employers.

In terms of the examination you should use version one unless the question instructs you otherwise.

5.5   Liquidity

A business can be highly profitable but if it is unable to pay its debts on the due dates it is in serious trouble. The term generally used to express this situation is insolvent. In the case of sole traders and partnerships proven insolvency could lead to the bankruptcy of the principals and, if the insolvency relates to a limited company, the company can be wound up (the company is put into liquidation). Essentially both these processes involve selling the assets of the debtor to repay the creditor. When presenting a petition for bankruptcy or winding up, the creditor (who must be owed at least £750) does so knowing that, unless he is fully secured, there is a strong possibility that the liquidation will not realize sufficient funds to repay the outstanding debt in full, but may result in some payment.

The rules covering bankruptcy are the Insolvency Act 1986 and the Insolvency Rules 1986, and *company liquidation* is covered by the Insolvency Act 1986. While both sole traders and partners are fully liable for all their business debts, the directors and shareholders of a company are protected by the separate legal existence of the company. In the past this has provided comfort to directors, some of whom took advantage and continued to permit a company to trade to their advantage but to the detriment of the creditors. This problem was addressed by Section 214 of the Insolvency Act. Under this section the directors can be held personally liable for the debts of the company if the director had allowed the company to continue trading when the director:

> *knew or ought to have concluded that there was no reasonable prospect that the company would avoid going into insolvent liquidation.*

In this scenario the director will have to prove that every step which ought to have been taken to minimize potential loss to creditors had been taken. There is an ancillary point for a lender to consider. Can the lender be considered to be acting as a director of the company? The legal term is *shadow director* and has been defined by the Act:

> *a person in accordance with whose instructions a company is accustomed to act.*[10]

Remember that the company, although a separate legal entity, interacts with the outside world via its directors. It is possible that a board of directors has such a good relationship with its account manager that they treat his suggestions as instructions and act accordingly. Under this scenario there is a possibility that the bank could be considered to be a shadow director and liable for losses to creditors under Section 214. This principle was almost tested in 1989[11] but the liquidator pulled back. There is still the possibility that a liquidator who felt his case was stronger might try to prove shadow directorship. Watch this space.

[10] Section 251 Insolvency Act 19986.
[11] *Re. M.C. Bacon.*

Given the importance of the liquidity how shall we measure it?

Working capital ratio	$\dfrac{\text{Current assets}}{\text{Current liabilities}}$
(Current Ratio)	

Acid test ratio	$\dfrac{\text{Current assets} - \text{Stock}}{\text{Current liabilities}}$
(Quick Ratio)	

Both of these ratios are attempting to ascertain the ease with which the company can utilize its current assets to meet current liabilities. Remember that the current assets are generally cash, stock and debtors while current liabilities are those debts due for payment in less than twelve months. These include trade creditors, overdrafts, and payments received on account. Neither of these definitions is complete.

These ratios are commonly used and there is a consensus that the working capital ratio should be in the region of 2:1 (current assets twice current liabilities) and the acid test ratio should not be less than 1:1 (current assets less stock equals current liabilities). The rationale behind the acid test ratio is that stock can be less liquid than cash or debtors and as such should be ignored. The usual caveats apply. A current ratio that is acceptable for one type of business will be unacceptable in another. Consider for example a supermarket. Its acid test ratio will reflect that fact that it has few, if any, debtors but it will have a substantial amount of its current assets in the form of stock. Alternatively a central heating firm might have a substantial debtor book but very limited stock.

5.6   Investment

All the previous ratios have been primarily geared towards potential lenders and the management of the business. The investment ratios, which are used for corporate businesses, are of major importance to the shareholders and potential shareholders.

The key investment ratios are:

Earnings per share	$\dfrac{\text{Profit after tax and preference dividends}}{\text{Number of ordinary shares in issue}}$

This figure can also be calculated as the *fully diluted earnings per share*. In this case the calculation assumes that all convertible loan stock, convertible preference shares and warrants have been converted to ordinary shares. Obviously the denominator is increased but this is offset to a greater or lesser extent by adding back to the earnings figure the interest and preference dividend paid.

This figure, expressed in pence per share, allows a shareholder to see exactly how much each share has theoretically earned him or her. The word theoretically is used because the company will not, as a general rule, give this to the shareholder as cash. The directors of the company will decide what proportion of the earnings needs to be kept in the business to allow the strengthening of the balance sheet, and how much needs to be paid as a dividend to meet the needs and expectations of the shareholders. In a private limited company this is a far less difficult balancing act than for a plc. Remember that the plc has its share traded on a stock exchange and these shares can be bought by anybody. Should the shareholders be consistently disappointed with the level of dividend they may react by selling their shareholding. If enough shareholders do this, the price of the share could fall making the company a takeover target.

The directors usually believe that the company has a better future as an independent concern rather than a subsidiary of BIGCO plc[12] and their dividend payment policy will reflect this and other factors. One of these factors is that the directors are probably shareholders as well. The dividend eventually paid will be approved by the shareholders at the annual general meeting.

Dividend per share

$$\frac{\text{Total dividend paid}}{\text{Number of shares}}$$

This is again expressed as pence per share and represents the actual payment made for every share held. Shareholders will convert this to:

Dividend yield

$$\frac{\text{Dividend per share}}{\text{Market price of share}}$$

This figure is expressed as a percentage and allows a comparison between the income received from the share and other investments.

Dividend cover

$$\frac{\text{Earnings per share}}{\text{Dividend per share}}$$

Expressed as a ratio this is a measure of the security of dividend payment. It should be remembered that there is *no* definitive link between earnings per share and dividend per share. The major concern would be if the cover were less than one. This means that the company has paid out more in dividends than it can afford to do based on the earnings for the year. This payment will have been made out of retained profits but this situation cannot continue for any great length of time.

Are ratios the answers to a lender's prayer?

We have just spent a long time considering the various ratios that can be calculated and have, hopefully, learned that trends across a number of years and comparisons with other businesses are far more important than a single year's figure in isolation. We have also begun to say that some ratios are more important than others and some ratios support, and are supported by, others and you should always be looking for supporting evidence for any conclusion drawn from a ratio. Conversely there will be times when some key ratios contradict each other. For example, a company may have shown a good growth in net profit margin (good sign) over

---

[12] The cynic might say that the directors are also concerned about their positions.

the last three years but an increase in credit taken and stock turnover period accompanied by a extension in credit given (bad signs). What do we do? We need to look *under* the figures and try to ascertain where the ratios have come from.

If we consider the example above, the net profit increase could be derived as follows:

	1998	1999
Sales	100,000	100,000
Cost of goods sold	82,000	72,000
Gross profit	18,000	28,000
Expenses	9,000	15,000
Net profit	9,000	13,000
Net profit margin	9 %	13 %

Yes, the net profit has increased, as has the net profit margin, but this has been because of a large decrease in the cost of goods sold. Could this be because of a change in stock valuation policy or perhaps a fall in the price of the cost of goods purchased?. The figures reveal two other aspects that would be of concern, the static sales and the 67% increase in the expenses of the business. These two worrying figures have been totally hidden by the fall in cost of goods sold. Suppose we recast the 1999 figures using the same cost of goods sold.

	1998	1999
Sales	100,000	100,000
Cost of goods sold	82,000	82,000
Gross profit	18,000	18,000
Expenses	9,000	15,000
Net profit	9,000	3,000
Net profit margin	9 %	3 %

Here the fall in net profit would be very disturbing. We would need to ascertain whether or not the reduced cost of the goods is a structural change in the market and will be a feature of future years trading. That would be good. Even so, the static sales and the increases in expenses are a major worry.

As we continue to look at ratios that concern us there are a few points to remember. Firstly consider that while the accounts purport to be highly accurate and precise they have been prepared using a number of estimations and interpretations. These need to be understood. Secondly they have been prepared to meet the needs of different users. It may very well be that the needs of a lending banker have been subordinated to the need to impress shareholders.

The third point is that the accounts are only a snapshot of the position of the business on a particular day – which will be months in the past. If there was a problem then what is the situation now?

Let us summarize the ratios in a table – which should certainly be committed to memory and look at Alfa Limited again.

Table 5.3

Capital Structure Ratios

Fixed assets/net worth

$$\frac{\text{Fixed assets}}{\text{Share capital + reserves}}$$

Net worth/total assets

$$\frac{\text{Share capital plus reserves}}{\text{Fixed and current assets}}$$

Gearing

$$\frac{\text{Long term debt}}{\text{Shareholders funds}}$$

$$\frac{\text{Long-term debt}}{\text{Shareholders funds + Long-term debt}}$$

Net gearing

$$\frac{\text{Total debt} - \text{Cash}}{\text{Shareholders' funds}}$$

Interest cover

$$\frac{\text{Profit before interest and tax}}{\text{Interest payable}}$$

Asset utilization ratios

Sales/fixed assets

$$\frac{\text{Sales}}{\text{Fixed assets}}$$

Stock turnover period

$$\frac{\text{Average stock}}{\text{Cost of sales}} \times 365$$

Debtor collection period

$$\frac{\text{Average trade debtors}}{\text{Credit sales}} \times 365$$

Creditor payment period

$$\frac{\text{Average trade creditors}}{\text{Credit purchases}} \times 365$$

Profitability

Gross profit margin

$$\frac{\text{Gross Profit}}{\text{Sales}} \times 100$$

Net profit margin

$$\frac{\text{Net Profit before interest and tax}}{\text{Sales}} \times 100$$

Operating margin

$$\frac{\text{Overheads}}{\text{Sales}} \times 100$$

Return on capital employed (ROCE)

$$\frac{\text{Profit before interest and tax}}{\text{Capital and reserves + Long-term liabilities}}$$

$$\frac{\text{Profit after tax}}{\text{Capital and reserves}}$$

Liquidity

Working capital ratio

$$\frac{\text{Current assets}}{\text{Current liabilities}}$$

Acid test ratio

$$\frac{\text{Current assets} - \text{Stock}}{\text{Current liabilities}}$$

Please note that we have not summarized the investment ratios.

Table 5.4: Alfa Ltd.

Trading and profit and loss account for the twelve months ended 5 April 1999

	Ratios			
Sales	**225,900**			
Cost of sales	(150,000)			
Gross Profit	**75,900**	GPM	75900/225900	33.60%
Distribution costs				
Administration costs	47,000	OM	47000/225900	20.81%
NPBT&I	**28,900**	NPM	28900/225900	12.79%
Interest payable	5,000	IC	28900/5000	5.78:1
Taxation	3,000			
NPAT&I	**20,900**			
Dividends	10,900			
Retained profit	**10,000**			

Table 5.5: Balance sheet as at 5 April 1999

Fixed Assets					Note
Freehold premises			45,000		1
Plant and machinery	Cost	20,000			
	Depreciation	5,000	15,000		2
Motor vehicles	Cost	12,000			
	Depreciation	2,000	10,000	70,000	
Current Assets					
Stock		21,000			3
Debtors		20,000			4
Bank		2,500	43,500		5
Current Liabilities					
Creditors		23,500	23,500		6
NET CURRENT ASSETS				20,000	7
Long-term liabilities					
Loan		(15,000)	(15,000)		8
TOTAL NET ASSETS				**75,000**	
Financed by					
50,000 £1 ordinary shares			50,000		9
Retained Profit			15,000		
Profit for the year			10,000		10
TOTAL NET ASSETS				**75,000**	

Sales/Fixed assets	225,900	= 3.22
Stock turnover	(21000/150000) x 365	= 51.10 d
Credit given	(20000/225900) x 365	= 32.32 d
Credit taken	(23500/150000) x 365	= 57.18 d
Current Ratio	43500/23500	= 1.85:1
Acid Test Ratio	(43500-21000)/23500	= 0.96:1
Gearing	(15000/75000) 100	= 20.00%
Net Gearing	15000-2500/75000 x 100	= 16.67%
ROCE	28900/(50000+25000+15000) x 100	= 32.11

Please check that you see where all the figures come from and keep the following in mind:

1. No average figures could be used for stock because only one year's figures are used

2. It was not possible to ascertain a credit purchase figure. What figure was used? Can you think why this was justified?

But what have we learnt about Alfa Ltd.? – Very, very little. Let us expand to look at ratios from the last four years.

Table 5.6: Ratios

	1996	1997	1998	1999	Trend	Interpretation
Gearing	52	38	29	20	Falling	Good: low borrowing
Net gearing	38.12	29.23	20.87	16.67	Falling	Good
Sales/Fixed assets	1.25	2.69	3.02	3.22	Rising	Fixed assets working harder
Stock turnover	125	98	78	51.1	Falling	Stock being sold more quickly
Credit given	69	56	40	32.32	Falling	Debts being collected more quickly
Credit taken	45	49	54	57.18	Rising	Being allowed to take longer credit
Gross profit margin	25	29	31	33.60	Rising	Getting prices for goods/services
Net profit margin	9	11	11.5	12.79	Rising	Controlling expenses
Operating margin	25	24	22	20.81	Falling	Controlling expenses
Interest cover	4.25	4.90	5.25	5.78	Rising	Interest becoming less of burden
Current ratio	1.60	1.79	1.80	1.85	Rising	Becoming more liquid
Acid test	0.5	0.75	0.78	0.96	Rising	Becoming less reliant on stock
ROCE	23.5	28.78	30.2	32.11	Rising	Better returns from capital

Let us take all the above ratios and see where (if anywhere?) they complement each other and where some concerns might be expressed.

Gearing

Both measures of gearing are falling. This is good in that borrowed funds place a strain on profitability and cash flow. This is especially true in times of high interest rates. The fact that interest cover is rising supports the falling gearing level. If the level of borrowing was falling but interest rates rising, then these ratios would be moving in opposite directions. One might argue that the low level of borrowing limits the possibility for growth for the business. However a good-quality business can always increase borrowing. Most lenders will calculate a projected gearing if substantial new lending is proposed. This practice is to be encouraged.

Suppose this business wanted to borrow an extra £35,000. This would make the projected gearing

$$\frac{15000 + 35000}{75000 + 35000} \qquad 45.5\%$$

This level of gearing is not one that would cause most lenders a problem. What would be of concern would be "What income is the extra £35,000 going to generate?" and "What will the projected interest cover be?" The business plan should address this point.

Sales/Fixed assets

Technically speaking every pound invested in fixed assets is producing more pounds of sales. One would expect to see increased sales and increased stock turnover.

Stock turnover

There is no evidence of obsolete stock here, which is good. If this falling ratio were seen with a falling gross profit margin there would be a suspicion that prices were being cut to generate sales. This may or may not be a problem. Reasons would need to be sought.

Credit given

A simple unambiguous ratio. The quicker the debts are collected the better.

Credit taken

As with debtors, a simple ratio to calculate but not quite so unambiguous. There are two possible reasons for the credit taken increasing. Firstly the company might be benefiting from lax credit control or a deliberately generous credit period granted by suppliers. Secondly, as stated earlier, the company might be deliberately holding back payment. Poor (and/or falling) current or acid test ratios would support the second scenario.

Gross profit margin (GPM)

This shows a higher mark-up. Hopefully this will be accompanied by increasing sales. Selling one item with a hundred per cent mark-up is not as good as selling five items with a twenty-five per cent mark-up. The gross profit margin can be manipulated by the method of calculating stock values and we should watch for this.

Net profit margin (NPM)

Hopefully increases in GPM will make their way through to the net profit. If they do not then the expenses are getting out of control. Nothing kills a business more quickly than poor expense control. Adverse movements in the current and acid test ratios often accompany falling NPM.

Operating margin (OM)

If the NPM is rising the OM must be falling. Many times this hides the fact that while overall expenses are in order, some individual expenses are of concern.

For example, wages might have risen substantially but the effect of this is masked by a fall in raw material costs. Go on – play with the figures. The danger here is obvious. Wages do not often go down but raw material prices can increase in price again.

Interest cover

Any lender wants a good interest cover. The figure we have for 1999 is telling us that profits for Alfa Ltd. can fall next year by almost eighty-three per cent[13] before the interest payment is threatened. A good interest cover also acts as a buffer against rising interest rates.

Current/Acid ratios

Normally never looked at separately. Although both are below the accepted normal levels of 2:1 and 1:1 respectively, neither of the ratios is a cause for concern. They are, in popular language, moving in the right direction. Remember that we know nothing of the business sector in which Alfa operates and these levels might be exceptionally good (or bad!) for this sector. Some say that while current and acid test ratios at low levels are danger signs, levels which are too high are also of concern. These may hide high levels of stock (obsolescence again – stock turnover again), high levels of debtors (potential bad debts – aged list of debtors?) or high levels of cash. Lots of cash is not always a good thing. Generally excess cash is earning nothing for the business. Surely something better could be done than leave it in bank accounts. Obviously a large discrepancy between the current ratio and acid test ratios shows a high element of stock. The stock in Alfa Ltd. forms almost 49% of the current assets. How does this compare with competitors? With Alfa Ltd. the good stock turnover mitigates some worries but perhaps the business is a little overstocked. Stock-control methods and ordering techniques are a subject in their own right. Some businesses keep a month's supplies in stock whereas others operate *Just In Time* (JIT) ordering. JIT keeps stock levels as close to zero as possible.

For Alfa Ltd. all the above ratios look excellent. The only concern would be "can this improvement be maintained?"

---

[13] $100 - (100/5.78)$.

6

GENERAL PRINCIPLES OF SECURITY

So far we have considered six out of seven of the *CAMPARI* framework:

Character   Is the borrower trustworthy?

Ability   Does the borrower have the necessary abilities to make the proposal successful?

Margin   How much risk does the proposal put the lender at and what is a fair interest premium for that risk?

Purpose   Is it legal, valid?

Amount   Is the amount requested too much, too little? How was it arrived at?

Repayment   What type of facility is required? Revolving credit or medium- or long-term loan? What will be the source of repayment?

In some cases the answers to all the above questions will be clear and unambiguous.

In such cases the facility will be granted on an unsecured basis. This means that if the clear and unambiguous information turns out to have been wrong the lender will have lost money and will need to either write off the indebtedness or seek repayment through the courts. Where there is some uncertainty in the answers[1] we may, as lenders, decide to take security for the facility. Taking security is *not* a substitute for proper assessment of the proposal (the risk) but rather a means of reducing the risk to a level that can be adequately rewarded by a reasonable interest. By this we mean that a proposal which might, on an unsecured basis, require a 4% above base rate can be granted at 3% above if suitable security was available. Again it must be stated that the availability of security does not make a sow's ear into a silk purse. We must always bear in mind that lending is a strange mix of art and science and that there is no simple formula which states that in cases A, B or C security must be taken.

Given that there are no rules for when to take security, when might we expect to see security taken? In personal lending situations we would normally expect security only taken in:

- house purchase;
- bridging loans.

In the majority of other personal lending situations it would not be normal to take security

[1] If you are uncertain about trustworthiness *do not* lend. This book is not called *Pawnbroking for Beginners*.

because the amounts are, in real terms, small and the costs involved in taking the security relatively large. However the primary reason why most personal lending is unsecured is because personal liability for debts is unlimited. If this point is unclear re-read Chapter 2 on customers.

Taking this thought on it should be becoming clearer that taking security in business situations is far more prevalent. The amounts involved are larger and thus potential losses greater and the cost of taking security more reasonable. The majority of business lending has some security involved.

So what is security? At the most basic level it is that which the borrower will give up to the lender in the event of default to compensate the lender for the losses incurred. Many assets can be used as security and these will be looked at in depth in Chapters 7 and 8. Briefly the most common assets are:

- land (including buildings);

- life policies;

- stocks and shares;

- guarantees;

- fixed and floating charges;

- goods and produce.

What does the above group have in common? They all have a value. Thus the loss would be a real cost to a borrower.

6.1 Security values

Security has two principal values and although we will primarily concentrate on the financial value we should be aware that some assets have a *value in use*. To illustrate what is meant by value in use let us recall the literary reference at the beginning of this book. We asked you to look at *The Merchant of Venice*. In this play a young man of poor means and uncertain character needed a loan. (The purpose was a little dicey too.) He was reduced to seeking funds from a moneylender who was considered a little outside the pale.

The lender was prepared to agree to the loan subject to a guarantee (a promise to repay) from a third party – a man of means and of good character (sound familiar?).

As an additional condition the lender asked for a further promise. That the guarantee should take the form of a pound (as in 450 grams) of the guarantor's flesh that would be forfeit if the loan was not repaid at a certain date. The lender reasoned that what could be of more value than a hand (or an arm or leg). The guarantor agreed. Although the pound of flesh had no monetary value it had infinite value in use and the loss would greatly distress the guarantor. We will return to the story soon.

Generally a lender seeks a form of security that can be valued in financial terms – because this can be related directly to the level of debt. The more easily and accurately the value of a security can be ascertained the better. One of the principle features of good security is that it is easy to value and that the value is stable or improving.

Let us return to Venice to ascertain another feature of good security. As one might expect (because otherwise there would be no story) things went wrong for both the debtor[2] and the guarantor, whose fortunes failed due to circumstances outside his control. The lender insisted on his cash repayment or his pound of flesh. A court case ensued and the court held in favour of the lender. Feature of good security two. Evidence that the asset has been given as security must be in such a form that it can be recognized by others and particularly by the legal authorities who will arbitrate on any dispute between the parties.

The best security will be that which lends (pardon the pun) itself to being registered and acknowledged by a party independent of the parties involved. For example, if land is taken as security this fact can be registered at the District Land Registry and such registration offers extra protection to the lender. We will look at this more in Chapter 7. In addition, for companies there is a legal requirement that all assets owned by the company that are given as security must be registered at Companies House. However, it is the responsibility of the lender to register the fact that a legal interest[3] exists.

A further principle of good security can also be illustrated from our ongoing story.

As we said the court held in favour of the moneylender and ruled that he could claim his pound of flesh provided:

1. He cut the flesh out himself and

2. He only took a pound otherwise...[4]

This left the moneylender in a quandary. Firstly he was a little squeamish and did not relish the act of cutting into the guarantor's arm. And how could he judge exactly a pound?

Feature of good security three. It must be easy to realize. It is all very well having a registered charge over a ship worth £1,000,000 if the ship left Southampton last week and nobody knows where it is.

Before we leave Venice we can draw a few more points from the story. The moneylender chose to demand the security from a third party[5] – thus the security was *third-party security*. The borrower therefore had nothing to lose directly if the security needed to be realized. Had he promised to forgo a pound of his flesh in the event of default he would have given *direct security*.

> *Question time: Do you think the borrower would have taken the risks he took if he had given the security directly?*

Today lenders are still able to take direct security (that is security owned by the borrower) or third-party security (security given by another on behalf of the borrower). Would it surprise

---

[2] But not totally – read it!
[3] Bear with me; we will discuss this shortly
[4] Read the book.
[5] Because of his better standing.

you to learn that direct security is the most favoured? It ties the borrower in more. When considering taking security every lender will be asking "What is this security worth to the lender both in monetary value and in use?"

Research time – have a look at some business situations in your branch and see how often a charge has been taken over the residential property. Note that often the financial value of this will be zero. You should be comfortable with why. You should also be comfortable with why much of this security will be third-party as opposed to direct.

Final point. The guarantor retained the use of his pound of flesh until the debt became due. This means that the borrower is not deprived of the use of the asset until default. Compare this with the aforementioned pawnbroking.

So to review. We have seen that good security has the following characteristics:

1. It has a financial value that is stable and simple to assess. If it has a value in use to the borrower so much the better.

2. It can be easily realized by the lender in the event of default.

3. The existence of the lender's rights over the asset should be clear to others.

It is to this third point that we need to give further consideration. How can a lender show to the world at large that the asset has been given as security in such a way that others will acknowledge it and, importantly, that the asset holder cannot repudiate the deal.

6.2   Forms of security

In Venice the word of the guarantor was sufficient on its own and for several centuries the dictum "my word is my bond" was a valid and trustworthy form of evidence. However today the financial world is far more complex (and perhaps more cynical) and all lenders require a tangible evidence of their rights over the security. There are three main forms of security which we shall look at in greater depth.

Pledge

A solemn promise to make an asset available to a lender at the lender's request

This form of security is very weak. It is very difficult to enforce and difficult to value. Furthermore it cannot be registered. A lender may have been given a pledge and subsequently find that the pledged asset has been sold. Because of the overall weakness of pledges lenders will not generally rely on them. In Chapter 8 we shall discuss fixed and floating charges (a form of security given by companies) and it is common for this form of security to incorporate a negative pledge. Under a negative pledge the borrower promises not to grant a legal mortgage over an asset pledged within the fixed and floating charge. Importantly this negative pledge can be registered at Companies House, thus giving notice to others that a particular asset is not available as security without the prior consent of the fixed and floating charge holder.

Lien

is the right to retain possession of the property of another in lieu of payment.

Although more substantial than a pledge, the lien is still an informal form of security and would only rarely form the whole security for a facility. Liens can be particular or general. The particular lien relates (surprisingly) to a particular debt. For example, if you run out of petrol and have no money you might leave your watch with a garage in return for a gallon of petrol. The garage would retain the watch until the petrol was paid for. The general lien relates to all monies owed and banks have a general right of lien under *Brandao v. Barrett* (1846). Items deposited in safe custody are exempt from the general lien. Notice that liens remove the asset from the borrower and are thus not usable by them.

One of the main strengths of the lien is that it takes priority over a charge taken subsequent to the lien.

Mortgage

A mortgage is the most common form of security taken by lending bankers and is a form of written evidence that the rights to the asset have been transferred from the borrower to the lender. A mortgage is created by the signing of a charge form by the owner of the asset. Once the charge form has been signed the following terminology is used:

Mortgagor –   *The person giving the security –* in direct security this is the borrower.

You may find it easy to remember that borrower and mortgagor both end with the letter R.

Mortgagee –   *The person holding the security –* this is the lender.

Not surprisingly the wording of the charge form differs for direct and third-party security. Many instances of invalid charges have occurred because the incorrect charge form has been signed. Often the lender takes the documents that prove ownership of the asset into possession at the same time as the charge form is signed. If we consider our list of assets we can expand it to show the documents of ownership.

1. Land (including buildings)   Land certificate or title deeds.

    (see Chapter 7)

2. Life policies   Policy document issued by insurer.

    (see Chapter 8)

3. Stocks and shares   Share certificate issued by company.

    (Chapter 8 will expand this)

4. Guarantees   Not applicable.

5. Fixed and floating charges   Not applicable

6. Goods and produce   Trade note/Invoice (see Chapter 8)

Given that the above documents prove ownership, a lender would need to ask questions if duplicate or replacement documents were proffered by the potential mortgagor. A little cynical reflection should help you understand why.

Research time: Does your employer have rules on duplicate documents of title?

There are two distinct forms of mortgage: *legal* and *equitable mortgages*.

A *legal mortgage* is created when:

1. The charge form is expressed to be "a legal mortgage".

2. In the case of land when the charge form creates a lease in favour of the mortgagee for an unlimited period. The technical term is "for a term absolute in years".

Whenever a third-party legal mortgage is taken it is essential that the mortgagor is given independent legal advice prior to completion. We shall look at examples in the following chapters but this independent advice is to ensure that the mortgagor is aware of his or her obligations, the extent of the obligations and to confirm that he or she enter into this contract free of any undue influence. This is especially important when the asset is in the name of Mr and Mrs Smith and the debt is in the name of either Mr or Mrs Smith.

An *equitable mortgage* is created when:

1. The charge form is not expressed to be by way of a legal mortgage.

And far, far more frequently when:

2. The title documents are deposited with the lender with the intention that they are security. The lender on most occasions will take a *memorandum of deposit* to confirm the intent. If land is the asset in question there *must* be written evidence of the intent.

    In the case of third-party security there must obviously be some form of written evidence to show whose debt the asset is being deposited to secure.

Generally the mortgagee seeks a legal mortgage because this gives the greatest level of security. The legal mortgage actually gives the mortgagee the right to sell the asset to repay the debt if the borrower is in default, even if the mortgagor objects. The mortgagee does not usually sell the asset if a borrower is a few days late in making a payment or a little in excess of a revolving credit facility. The action of repossessing an asset under a legal mortgage is always the last, as opposed to the first, course of action.

Generally the mortgagee seeks to explore all other possible avenues with the mortgagor before issuing a notice requiring repayment of debt. This formal notice is a legal requirement[6]. From the date of service of this notice the borrower has three months before the asset can be sold. This time period can be a distinct disadvantage for a lender and generally Section 103 of the Law of Property Act (1925) is excluded, making the debt repayable on demand.

A mortgagee can also sell the security if interest is two months in arrears or if the borrower has broken some other condition of the loan. These conditions are often referred to as

---

[6] Law of Property Act 1925 (Sec. 103).

covenants. An example of a covenant is that the borrower must forward monthly management accounts to a lender and that the overdraft is limited to an amount related to the working capital. And many facilities offered by lenders will contain one or more covenants.

Research time: How many different coventants can you think of?

An equitable mortgage does not give the mortgagee the right to sell the asset against the wishes of the mortgagor without the permission of the court. This is expensive, time consuming and not 100% guaranteed. Another major disadvantage of the equitable mortgage is that the mortgagee will rank behind any prior equitable mortgages even if they were unaware of them at the time the mortgage was created.

For example

On 15 March Mr Smith borrowed £40,000 from Abbey West Bank plc and gave an equitable mortgage over £45,000 worth of shares. After default the bank receives permission to enforce the sale of the shares and confidently expects to receive enough to repay the debt and unpaid interest. Unfortunately it transpires that the shares are already subject to an equitable mortgage on January 23. This prior charge takes precedence over its mortgage.

If the prior mortgage was in favour of Alla Bank, which is owed £25,000, the following would be the situation facing Abbey West.

	£
Sale proceeds	45,000 (ignore charges)
Repay Alla Bank	28,500 (debt plus unpaid interest)
Available to Abbey West	16,500

Thus Abbey West is facing a shortfall of £24,500 (plus any unpaid interest). Effectively Abbey West had a second mortgage – that is, their rights were subject to the overriding rights of a first mortgagee.

If Abbey West had taken a legal mortgage on 15 March its rights would have taken precedence over those of Alla Bank and Alla Bank would have been left with the shortfall.

Had Alla Bank taken the legal mortgage then Abbey West would have had knowledge of this.[7] Abbey West may still decide to make facilities available to Mr Smith but at a far lower level.

	£
Value of shares	45,000
At 80%	36,000
Level of debt of Alla Bank	28,500
Value in the security	7,500

[7] The non-existence of a share certificate or a duplicate certificate would cause enquires to be made to the company registrar, who would be able to confirm the prior charge of Alla Bank.

In most cases of first and second mortgages the two lenders agree a deed of priorities between them in order to take interest into account. In simple terms, Alla Bank agrees that it will have priority for the original debt plus £X interest. X may be expressed as a number of months interest or a specific amount of interest.

There may even be a third and fourth mortgagee!! In many cases the second mortgagee will have taken the mortgage simply to lock the borrower in. A usual scenario would be a company seeking to borrow from its bank. The company is owned by and run by the directors. As part of the security package the lender may want a guarantee from a director supported by a second mortgage over the director's domestic residence.

It may very well be that the domestic property is worth £140,000 and the subject of a first mortgage to Beta Building Society for £125,000. The value in the mortgage would be zero.

	£
Value	140,000
% 90%	126,000
First mortgage	125,000
Value to second mortgagee	nil – the 1000 will be taken in charges

As we have talked about charge forms it is appropriate to consider the clauses that typically appear in such a document and there is a mnemonic to aid memory.

CASCAR (See-A-Scar)

C: Continuing security

The effect of this clause is that the security continues (remains) valid notwithstanding that the original money lent has been repaid.

The easiest way to see this is in the case of a revolving credit facility. Let us assume that an overdraft of £20,000 has been granted and the borrower has taken (drawn down) the funds. Subsequently the customer pays in £5,000 per month and withdraws £4,750.

After five months the following has happened:

Table 6.1

	Credits	Debits	Balance
			20000 dr.
	5000	4750	19750 dr.
	5000	4750	19500 dr.
	5000	4750	19250 dr.
	5000	4750	19000 dr.
Total in/out	20000	19000	

Within the four months the £20,000 borrowed has been paid back in. It could, therefore, be argued that the four tranches of £5,000 have repaid the original amount. **How does this argument seem to you?**

In 1816 the issue was considered in *Clayton's Case* and the court held that the argument was valid. Therefore in the above case although the balance on the current account was £19,000 the security had ceased to be valid.

To overcome the rule in *Clayton's case* all charge forms now incorporate a *continuing security clause* in the following terms:

> ... *a continuing security and shall extend to cover the **ultimate** balance due from the customer to the lender notwithstanding the fact that the customer may have had, from time to time, a credit balance on an account between the customer and the lender.*

If the charge form had incorporated the continuing security clause then the balance of £19,000 would have been covered by the charge form and the security would remain valid. This would still be the case if the customer had gone into credit for x months and then become overdrawn again.

A: All monies

Under this clause the customer promises to pay on demand *"all monies now due or hereafter due to the lender"*. Effectively the customer acknowledges that this security covers all monies owed on any account of the customer's at any time. The practical implication is that if a customer who owed £100,000 and had given two items of security each worth £55,000 subsequently repaid £50,000 of the debt then the lender can keep both items of security even though the debt has halved. The customer cannot demand the release of one of the items of security, although in many cases the lender will often be willing to release one of the items of security, perhaps in conjuncture with reducing the facility. The downside of such a release for the customer is that if he or she wished to increase the facility back to the £100,000 level there would be a delay and cost involved with retaking the security.

S: *Successor*

This clause enables the lender's rights under the security to be transferred to a third party who might take over the bank's rights. This clause would be very important if the much rumoured take-over by clearing bank A of clearing bank B takes place.

C: *Conclusive evidence*

This clause has the effect that if the bank sends a statement showing the debt to be £X and this statement is not disputed within fourteen days then £X is the binding level of debt. This effectively prevents any dispute over the amount of the debt.[8]

A: *Additional security*

> *This security is in addition to and without prejudice to **any** other security now or at any time held.*

This effectively means that the lender can take, or release, other security without having an effect on the security.

R: *Repayment on demand*

We have already seen that by excluding Section 103 of the Law of Property Act 1925 the lender obtains the right to demand repayment immediately.

This Act, although almost 75 years old, is a pivotal piece of legislation and we have seen that Section 103 must be excluded to give the repayment on demand clause validity. Similarly Section 93 must be excluded to validate the all monies clause. However, the power to sell under a legal mortgage is granted by Section 101 of the Act. Before leaving the Law of Property Act we should finally say that the term *property* means all assets owned by an individual (or company) and not just land.

To date we have looked at security and not considered whether it is owned by an individual, partnership or company. The reason for this is that it does not matter. All three can own property, although partnership property is deemed jointly owned by all partners only if it was purchased with partnership money.

The only difference is in the case of a fixed and floating charge, which is a form of security that can only be created by a limited company. This will be discussed further in Chapter 8.

Before moving into specific types of security in Chapters 7 and 8 we need to look at the time when security comes into its own. When a company (or personal) facility is progressing nicely then security is of no concern. It is when a company goes into liquidation – or an individual goes into bankruptcy – that security becomes of value and investigation of the security is undertaken by the liquidator (or trustee in bankruptcy). Remember that it is the liquidator's function to realize the assets of the company and pay the creditors. He or she

---

[8] There is a possibility that the Unfair Contracts Terms Act (1977) might in some cases invalidate this clause.

will do this in the following set pattern:

1. Creditors with legal charges – any excess funds generated by selling the security go to the liquidator and shortfall becomes unsecured.

2. Liquidator's expenses.

3. Preferential creditors – tax, national insurance, VAT, pension contributions, wages (up to £800 per employee).

4. Floating-charge holders.

5. Unsecured creditors.

6. The owners.

Every liquidator wants to investigate any security document seeking any flaws in the security-taking process that make the security invalid and thus bring the asset into the total "pot" available for the liquidator to distribute.

For example

Table 6.2

	Debt	Security
Creditors with legal charges	100,000	100,000
Liquidator's expenses	20,000	
Preferential creditors	20,000	
Floating-charge holders	10,000	10,000
Unsecured creditors	160,000	
	310,000	110,000
The total assets are £200,000		
	200,000	
Less legal charge	100,000	
Less floating charge	10,000	
Available to liquidator	90,000	
Less liquidation expenses	20,000	
	70,000	
Preferential creditors	20,000	
Available to unsecured creditors	50,000	

Thus each unsecured creditor would receive

$$\frac{50,000}{160,000} = 31.25 \text{ pence in the pound}$$

What if the liquidator were able to find a flaw in the security of the fixed-charge holder which the court upheld, thus invalidating the security? The situation would become:

Table 6.3

	Debt	Security
Creditors with legal charges	100,000	
Liquidator's expenses	20,000	
Preferential creditors	20,000	
Floating-charge holders	10,000	10,000
Unsecured creditors	160,000	
	310,000	110,000

The total assets are £200,000.

	200,000
Less floating charge	10,000
Available to liquidator	190,000
Less liquidation expenses	20,000
	170,000
Preferential creditors	20,000
Available to unsecured creditors	150,000
Unsecured creditors	260,000 (the 100,000 becomes unsecured)

Thus each unsecured creditor would receive

$$\frac{150,000}{260,000} = 57.69 \text{ pence in the pound}$$

The invalid legal charge holder would receive £56,692 as opposed to the £100,000 it would have received had the security been valid. In light of this it is not exaggerating to say that a flaw in taking security can have drastic consequences for a lender.

The liquidator will be looking for three main types of flaws:

Technical

- Does the borrower have the capacity to contract?

- Has the charge form been properly completed?

- Are the signatures witnessed?

- Was independent legal advice given?

- Was notice give to prior mortgagees?

- Has the charge been registered correctly? This is extremely important with company borrowing.

This is not an exhaustive list and you should examine the security documentation procedures of your employer. Many of these will be in the form of a flow chart to ensure that all technicalities are correctly completed.

Preference

It is illegal to prefer one creditor ahead of the others and were a debtor to do so the liquidator could ask the court to reverse the preference transaction. For example, if a lender was an unsecured creditor and then was given security shortly before the debtor went bust, the liquidator would seek to claim preference and have the security brought back into the distribution, with the lender reverting to an unsecured creditor. The court will consider the time between the granting of the security and the insolvency of the mortgagor.

In the ordinary course of events the claim of preference is avoided if six months have passed since the creation of the mortgage. If the mortgagee was an associate of the debtor (spouse, company director preferred by a company, etc.), the timescale increases to two years.

Transactions under value

This is were the debtor has transferred an asset to a creditor (or other third party) for less than its market value. This effectively means that there is less value available to the creditors in insolvency.

In *Aveling Barford Ltd v. Perion Ltd* (1989) the liquidator of Aveling Barford successfully petitioned the court to force Perion to repay over £1,000,000 after an asset owned by Aveling Barford to Perion had been sold substantially under value. The link between the two companies was a common major shareholder.

The timescale for transactions under value is two years for a company and five years for individuals.

7

LAND

Land, and anything permanent on it[1], is the most popular form of security in the UK, and it is reasonable to assume that this will continue to be the norm for many years to come. For our purposes the term land can mean farming land, commercial land[2] or domestic land[3], and we shall not differentiate between these unless it becomes absolutely necessary.

Let us for a moment return to the works of the Bard. Richard III was reported to have said:

> *A horse! a horse! my kingdom for a horse!*

This pitiful cry was not the offer of the best swap deal for centuries but rather signified the fact the Richard felt that his kingdom might be lost because of the need of a horse.

Similarly in a more modern context many lenders have paraphrased and cried:

> *Land! land! my facility for land!*

And sadly this cry was often heeded in the late 1980s and early 1990s and many lenders granted facilities that did not stand up on CAMPARI purely because the security offered was land (or land and buildings). It could be argued that the art of lending was forgotten during this period and the 'art'? of pawnbroking took over.

> *Research Time – pick up a copy of your employer's annual report for between 1992-1995 and see how much was written off because of overreliance on property values.*

Why then do all lenders want land as security? If we think back to the features of good security discussed in Chapter 6, land does indeed stand up well. Generally speaking land has the following advantages as security:

1. Ownership is generally simple to establish – The title will be evidenced by either a land certificate or by title deeds and documents[4].

2. A valuation is generally simple to obtain – There are two main professional bodies that carry out valuations on all types of land. These will give their independent opinion of the possible selling price of the land and, although they are not guaranteeing the value, their track record, as a profession, is very good. Most lenders will also have their own personal experience to draw upon.

---

[1] Buildings and crops.
[2] Land with shops, factories, etc. on it.
[3] Surprise, surprise – this type of land has houses on it.
[4] Both of these will be discussed in greater depth later.

3. The legal charge is easily evidenced by a mortgagee. The landowner will sign (or with a company, seal) the charge form and this will incorporate the standard clauses considered in Chapter 6. We shall look at the actual procedure for taking land as security later in the chapter. The charge form then becomes part of the title deeds or is recorded by the District Land Registry. Again we shall discuss this in more detail later.

4. There is normally a ready market for land and sales can normally be achieved within a reasonable timeframe. However, the experience of the late 1980s and early 1990s when land values actual fell (and in some cases substantially) has scarred lenders badly. Many lenders often ask for two values from the valuer.

   - *Open Market Valuation*. This is based on a ready market and a willing buyer and a willing seller.

   - *Forced Sale Valuation*. This basically restricts the valuer to assessing what price will be obtained within a fixed timeframe, which could be 30, 60 or 90 days. Obviously the price obtained if the land had to be sold within 30 days would be far less than if 90 days were available to find a buyer.

On the downside land has few disadvantages.

1. The security procedure can be complicated and time-consuming. There a lot of "Is" to be dotted and "Ts" to be crossed. Mistakes in the technicalities can invalidate the security. There will be, within your circle of colleagues, a horror story to support this.

2. Valuers do not guarantee their valuations, and factors beyond the control of lenders – such as recession – can greatly reduce the expected returns. The term *negative equity* (now thankfully become increasingly rare) refers to the state where a mortgagor owes the mortgagee more than the security is worth. Thus selling the asset still leaves a residual debt.

3. Much of the value is often based on the fixtures on the land, i.e. the buildings. Although the land cannot be destroyed (other than by Act of God), the buildings can burn down, be blown up or simply be allowed to fall into disrepair. Although a lender cannot force a mortgagor to keep the property up to a certain level of repair, it can insist that the building is insured against fire, flood, etc. The cost of this insurance is normally borne by the customer but the lender may have to pay the insurance premiums if the customer is in difficulty.

4. Land can be difficult to sell. Even with the right to sell incorporated into the standard charge form (and discussed in Chapter 6), if nobody wants to buy there is no sale. In addition to the potential difficulty in selling there are always ancillary costs to be considered; legal fees, estate agent fees, etc. will all reduce the amount the mortgagee will receive.

Footnote 4 promised that we would consider the ownership of land in greater detail later. Well later is here.

7.1   Land ownership

All land historically belongs to the Crown but the Law of Property Act 1925 begins (Section 1) by stating that two legal estates in land can be created which are subject only to the rights of the Crown.

These legal estates are freehold and leasehold and the *Oxford Pocket Dictionary* defines these as follows:

Freehold	Complete ownership of property for an unlimited period.
Leasehold	Ownership of property by lease.

Lease – *contract by which the owner of property allows another to use it for a specified period, usually in return for payment.*

These ownerships can be either sole or joint and, as nothing yet has been straightforward, we need to consider the differences in the types of joint ownership. The first is *joint tenancy*. Under this type of ownership the land is deemed to be owned in full by both parties[5] and on the death of either the full title passes to the survivor. The alternative is *tenants in common*, under which each owner is deemed to own a portion of the land. On death this portion does not pass to the other tenant but to the heirs of the deceased tenant. The heir may, however, be the other tenant.

To be more formal than the *OPD* (which we must) the terms are defined as follows:

Freehold	Fee simple absolute in possession.
Fee	The land can be inherited.
Simple	The land can be inherited by the closest heir.
Absolute	The land is owned unconditionally.
Possession	The owner has use of the land or benefits from the rent received from the lease.

Thus freehold land is owned unconditionally and the ownership passes to the closest heir on the death of the owner. The term of ownership is not limited and ceases only when the land is sold. The sale is called a *conveyance*.

Leasehold	**Term of years absolute**
Term of Years	The leaseholder has use of the land for a specified period.
Absolute	The land is owned unconditionally and does not cease on death. The rights under the lease pass to the heir on death. The lease can be sold to a third party. Such a sale is by way of an *assignment*. Usually the head lease does not prohibit such transfers but may hold certain restrictions.

It should be clear that whereas there can be freehold land without leasehold, there cannot be a leasehold without a freeholder.

[5] The Law of Property Act 1925 allows for up to, but not exceeding, four joint owners.

Any freeholder can grant a lease over his or her land by entering into a formal agreement called a *head lease*. The head lease defines the period of the lease, the rent due under the lease and the rights and obligations of the leasee (the leaseholder). Some leases make the leasee responsible for repairs, insurance, etc. of the property, while others leave these responsibilities with the leasor (freeholder). Most leases detail a set period for rent review and perhaps a pre-agreed mechanism for such a renewal.

For example, a common condition in head leases is the prohibition on the creation of a sub-lease. This is a clause preventing the leasee creating a further lease in favour of a third party.

Both freehold and leasehold are types of ownership of land. There are a number of other legal *interests* in land which are, effectively, rights to the land, but which are not ownership. The most widely known is the *right of way*. Under rights of way members of the public have the right to walk across the land without the permission of the freeholder. A mortgage is a legal interest in land which is of primary importance, and both freeholders and leaseholders can create mortgages over their particular estate. Obviously any lender taking a mortgage over leasehold land would examine the head lease very closely to ascertain any potential problems. For example, if a loan is granted for 20 years and the lease expires after 15 years what happens? Is the mortgage effective against the freeholder? *Nope!* Once the land reverts to the freeholder his rights are unaffected by any interests created by the lessee. This is an important point. A leaseholder cannot bind the freeholder.

As we discussed in Chapter 6, it is important that a lender knows who owns an asset and what his or her rights over that asset are. The type of estate defines the rights but we still need to consider the means of confirming ownership.

Both freehold and leasehold land can be either unregistered title or registered title. Unregistered title is the most cumbersome whereas registered is very simple. For unregistered title a bundle of deeds and documents will exist which show the chain of ownership as shown in the example below.

Table 7.1

Date	Document	From	To	Note
14 June 1878	Conveyance	S. Smith	J. Jones	1
20 May 1900	Head lease	J. Jones	S. Stevens 99 years	2
15 March 1945	Assignment	S. Stevens	T. C. Parry	3
5 Oct 1950	Conveyance Freehold Est.	J. Jones	T. C. Parry	4
6 Feb 1975	Conveyance	T. C. Parry	L. M. Willams	5
6 Feb 1975	Mortgage	L. M. Williams	Middlys Bank Ltd.	6
6 Feb 1990	Mortgage	Middlys Bank Ltd.	L. M. Williams	7

Notes:

1. S. Smith has sold has freehold estate to J. Jones (who becomes the new freeholder).

2. J. Jones creates a head lease lasting for 99 years. After the expiry the full ownership reverts to J. Jones.[6]

3. S. Stevens assigns the remaining period (54 years) of his lease.

4. T. C. Parry has purchased the freehold estate from the heirs of J. Jones. Effectively T. C. Parry has recombined the freehold and leasehold estate, and any restrictions within the head lease do not apply to him or those to whom he may sell the land.

5/6 T. C. Parry has sold the property to L. M. Williams, who has borrowed money from Middlys Bank. The loan is secured by a mortgage. The bank has a legal interest in the land while L. M. Williams retains the legal estate. Middlys will retain the title deeds with their mortgage form. Any second mortgagee would not have the comfort of the deeds but would be able to register his or her interest at the land charges department as a class C puisne mortgage. This registration would be effective notice to any third mortgagees. There are several other classes of mortgage.

Research time – have a look in a law textbook.

7. The mortgage has been repaid and Middlys has discharged its mortgage form and thus their legal interest has ceased.

When L. M. Williams comes to sell (convey) the property, the purchaser's solicitor (or licensed conveyancer) will inspect the documents to ensure that a good title can be obtained by the buyer. Imagine that T. C. Parry had not purchased the freehold in 1950; then he would have been able to assign only a leasehold estate to L. M. Williams. This interest would expire in 1999 and after that use of the land would revert to the heirs of J. Jones. Any purchaser after 1990 would base the purchase price on the fact that he or she would only have use of the property for nine years.

The conveyancer would also want to check the status of all legal interests – such as the mortgage. Any purchaser in 1986 would want confirmation, in addition to L.M. Williams conveying the freehold, that Middlys would confirm that their mortgage over the land would be discharged. This would normally be achieved by the solicitor for L.M. Williams undertaking to forward sufficient funds from the sale proceeds to discharge the mortgage debt. The purchaser would then have good title subject, of course, to any mortgage arrangements made to purchase the land.

Although the example shows only seven stages, it is not unusual for there to be many more both in terms of conveyances, assignments and discharged mortgages and the title chain can be difficult to follow, especially if some of the documents are old or have been damaged. In practice a good chain of title can be established over a 15-year period and defective title indemnity can be purchased from an insurance company to protect against defects in title that may appear in later years.

[6] Or his heirs or assignees.

Thoughtful readers may be querying why the estate of J. Jones sold the freehold estate in 1945 when the title was due to revert in 1999. In all probability the heirs took the view that the rent received under the terms of the lease (called the *ground rent*) was very small and they would rather have a capital sum today than £1.50 p.a. for the next 54 years. Under the Leasehold Reform Act 1967 a leaseholder has the right to force the freeholder to sell the freehold, and while this is reasonably common in domestic situations, it is not widely applicable commercially.

As stated above, the title deeds for unregistered land can be very cumbersome and there have been many occasions were it has proved difficult to ascertain, with absolute certainty, the true ownership. This is not the case with registered land.

The Land Registration Act of 1925 established a framework whereby title to land could be registered at one of a number of District Land Registries (DLR). These can be seen as a DVLA for property. Just as the DVLA keeps a record of the registered keepers of motor vehicles and issues a logbook showing the name and address of said keeper, so the DLR keeps records of the owners of land. Initially the DLR inspects the title deeds and documents (to prove title) and then issues a land certificate to the owner. This certificate has an alphabetic prefix[7] and a numeric suffix, e.g. WA76583. This is unique to the land, which might be better known to its owners as 14 Paradise Gardens, Angeltown HE4 3AN. The certificate includes a map showing (with red etching) the extent of the land covered and is valid in boundary disputes.

Most land is now in compulsory registration and any purchaser of the land owned by L.M. Williams would receive a land certificate as proof of title. The new owner would also receive the pre-registration deeds and documents but these, while historically fascinating, are of no financial value. A land certificate is issued for freehold or leasehold land and usually the land certificate for leasehold land incorporates the head lease.

From a mortgagee's point of view a land certificate is wonderful. It guarantees ownership. If it transpires that title is/was defective, the government will recompense those suffering from the mistake of the DLR. But more importantly, once a mortgage has been created the DLR will register this (on the Charges Registry) and issue the mortgagee with a charge certificate while retaining the land certificate. Thus the mortgagor has no evidence of title (other than a receipt from the mortgagee) and is thus unable to create a further mortgage without the mortgagee's consent. However, a second mortgagee will be able to obtain the benefit of a charge certificate in his or her favour when a second mortgage is created.

When the land is sold the existing entries are ruled through and new entries made.

If we consider the chain of title in the example above, we will see that item six was the mortgage between Middlys and L.M. Williams. It would benefit us all to take a journey through the procedure, because as shown in Chapter 6, any defect in taking the security can invalidate the security.

---

[7] Wales, for example, is WA.

7.2   Procedure for taking security

Stage 1 – Obtain a valuation on the land

The valuer needs to be professionally qualified and familiar with the geographical area concerned. A London-based valuer would experience difficulties assessing the value of a property in the highlands of Scotland. The basis of the valuation should be clearly set. Is the valuer to assess on an open-market or forced-sale basis? Would both be appropriate?

Stage 2 – Obtain the deeds or land certificate

The availability of the title documents is a good indication that there are no charges on the land, but an equitable charge may still exist. Searches at the Land Charges Department (unregistered land) and the District Land Registry (registered land) should be undertaken to ensure that no such charges exist. If they did they would take precedence over the legal mortgage.

For unregistered land it is essential that the chain of title is investigated and proven. Some financial institutions do this in house whereas others use solicitors.

Stage 3 – Execute the mortgage form

The mortgage form must obviously be signed. It is at this stage that a number of problems can occur.

- Are all the owners of the property signing the document? Is the land in joint tenancy or tenants in common? Think how tenancy in common might affect the mortgagee's position.

- Is the owner the borrower? If yes, then a direct charge form will be used. If the owner is not the borrower a third-party charge form would be needed.

- Are there any parties with an equitable interest in the land? For example, does the person buying the property have a partner who will live in the property as well? The rights of a partner living in, and contributing[8] to the property, were defined in *Williams and Glyn Bank Ltd. v. Borland* (1980). Here Mr Borland was the registered owner and mortgaged the marital home. The court held that the bank was unable to obtain possession because Mrs Borland had an overriding equitable interest.

   The practical implication of *Williams and Glyn Bank Ltd. v. Borland* (1980) is that all lenders will seek the consent to the mortgage of all occupants of a property whose name(s) do *not* appear on the title deeds. This applies only to those persons in occupation at the date of execution of the charge form.

   The ruling in *Borland* has been revisited in (amongst others) *Midland Bank Ltd. v. Dobson* (1985), *City of London Building Society v. Flegg* (1986) and *Lloyds Bank plc v. Rossett* (1990) and, while clarifications have been made, the underlying principle remains valid.

---

[8] The contribution need not be in terms of money.

Further equitable rights are given to a deserted spouse under the Matrimonial Homes Act (1983). This act gives such a spouse the right to occupy the matrimonial home for as long as the marriage lasts. The deserted spouse would need to register his or her interest at either the *Land Charges Department* or the *District Land Registry (DLR)*. Spouses can further protect their position by advising the mortgagee of their interest so that their equitable interest will rank ahead of future lending by the mortgagee.

- Have all parties had independent legal advice? We will consider *Lloyds Bank Ltd. v. Bundy* (1975) and *Barclays Bank plc v. O'Brien* (1993) in Chapter 8. Both of these cases deal with the need for independent legal advice when giving security.

- With registered land, the land certificate and charge form must be forwarded to the relevant DLR, which will exchange it for a charge certificate.

Stage 4 – Search the local council records

This is done to ensure that there are no plans affecting the property. These might be local government plans or planning consents given to private concerns. For example, is the local authority planning to put a new road or motorway exit on derelict land adjacent to the security? Or are there plans to build a new school and leisure centre close to the land? While the mortgagee can do nothing about these plans, their existence could have a bearing on the valuation. If the security were a commercial property, a new road and motorway access may well increase the value. If the property is a residential property then the same plans could have a detrimental affect. If the local authority search reveals any such plans they should be discussed with the valuer to see if they change the valuation. It could be argued that a good valuer would be aware of these plans and will have incorporated them into the valuation already.

Stage 5 – Obtain the insurance policy

The policy document covering the land should be inspected to ensure that the land is properly and adequately insured and the policy document should be retained. It is normal for lenders to advise the insurer of their interest in the same. The insurance company then notes the lender's interest on the policy document. This means that in the event of non- payment of premiums the lender would be advised, enabling it to make the payments, thus keeping the security valid.

Summary of Procedure for taking a charge over land:

Stage One	Obtain a valuation on the land.
Stage Two	Obtain the deeds or land certificate.
Stage Three	Execute the mortgage form.
Stage Four	Search the local council records.

Stage Five   Obtain the insurance policy.

If a second mortgage were to be taken the procedure would be a little different. Obviously the primary difference is that the title documents are not available – because the first mortgagee will have them. Thus the first step a second (or third etc.) mortgagee would take would be to obtain details of the debt secured by the first mortgage. Each financial institution has a standard questionnaire which incorporates a mortgagor's authority to disclose the information requested. If the questionnaire is received without this authority the duty of confidentiality prevents disclosure.

On receipt of the completed questionnaire the second mortgagee has the following important details:

1. Confirmation of the name(s) of the landowners.

2. The amount of the outstanding debt. This will allow the second mortgagee to calculate the value of the security. This will be the value of the asset less normal reduction less amount owed to the first mortgagee.

3. Any obligation on the first mortgagee to make further advances. If such an obligation exists, these advances would take preference over the second mortgage even if the further advance were drawn down after the second mortgage. This can be overcome by a deed of priorities.

4. Details of any mortgages granted by third parties to the mortgagor. For example, there may already be a second mortgage in place. The existence of charges created subsequent to the first mortgage can also be ascertained by searching the Land Charges Department and District Land Registry.

Once the lender is satisfied as to the above points, the charge form can be signed (all the considerations detailed under stage three above will apply) and notice of the mortgage sent to the first mortgagee. The first mortgagee will confirm the level of debt outstanding and any further lending by the first mortgagee will rank after the second mortgage (barring, of course, any further advances made under the obligations discussed in 3. above).

Because the title deeds are held by the first mortgagee, the charge of the second mortgagee needs to be registered. For unregistered land this will be by way of a Class c(1)[9] at the Land Charges Department and, for registered land, the charge form will be forwarded to the relevant DLR and exchanged for a charge certificate. In the case of unregistered land the mortgagee would search the land charges department a second time to ensure that the second mortgage has been registered.

It would be prudent to check with the local authority as in stage four above. Stage five is probably unnecessary, because the first mortgagee will have done this. It can, however, do no harm to check.

The above stages for taking first and second mortgages are generalist only and different financial institutions have specific programmes for ensuring that all the technicalities are

---

[9] Puisne mortgage.

correctly completed.

The last 1,300 words have dealt with the correct taking of security over land, so let us see what options are available to the mortgagee if the loan (which is supported by the mortgage) goes wrong. As with much of what we have considered there is a simple mnemonic to assist students to remember the possibilities.

SAFES[10]

This stands for:

Sue

A lender can sue independently of the security it holds if it so desires. This is rare and would indicate that the lender believes that there may be a fault in its security or that the security has fallen to little value.

Appoint a receiver

This procedure is generally used where the property is not occupied by the borrower but by tenants. The receiver is then entitled to receive the rent instead of the borrower. An important consideration would be the level of the rent compared to the costs of the mortgage.

Foreclosure

This procedure which must be approved by the court. Under foreclosure, ownership of the property is transferred to the lender regardless of the amount of debt compared with the value of the property. Lenders rarely attempt this procedure because it is time-consuming, expensive and unlikely to succeed.

Enter into possession

Basically this involves the lender evicting the borrower from the property. Again this needs court approval (again incurring time and expense). If the court approves the possession (by no means certain!) the lender becomes a mortgagee in possession and as such becomes responsible for the upkeep and insurance of the property until it is sold. The court may decline to allow the possession for a time to allow the borrowers time to find a buyer themselves. The logic here is that an occupied property is more attractive to potential buyers than an empty property which a buyer would know the lender needed to sell.

Sell

If the property is occupied by the borrower(s) – which is the most common situation – then the lender has the right to sell the property against the wishes of the borrower. In the event of a sale the lender has a duty to obtain a fair price[11] and account to other mortgagees and the owner for any surplus received. Any lender selling under the power within the charge form would need to search the land charges department or district land registry to ascertain whether

---

[10] A contemporary of mine preferred FASES.
[11] *Standard Chartered Bank v. Walker and Walker.*

or not there are second (or third) mortgagees. This caused a number of problems during the late 1980s and early 1990s when lenders lent 95-100% (and occasionally more!!) of the purchase price in the expectation that the massive increase in land (and property) prices seen in the early 1980s would continue unabated[12]. The outcome was that when property values peaked and then fell sharply, many lenders, especially second mortgagees, were left with debts that exceeded the value of the security. The lender would rarely lose out by selling quickly because the mortgage guarantee indemnity would meet the shortfall, but the borrower was often left with no property, none of the equity it had originally invested and a debt to the indemnifier.

---

[12] Another example of the availability heuristic.

8

OTHER FORMS OF SECURITY

Having considered the best form of security in Chapter 7, it will be instructive to look at the other assets that may be offered in addition to land or as an alternative.

These primarily consist of:

1. A fixed and floating charge.

2. Life policies.

3. Stocks and shares.

4. Guarantees and indemnities.

5. Goods and produce.

8.1 Fixed and floating charges

This form of security is restricted to companies and is not available to individuals or partnerships. A fixed and floating charge consists of two distinct elements. Specifically these are:

A fixed charge over book debts (*Siebe Gorman & Co. Ltd. v. Barclays Bank Ltd.* (1979))

Together with

A floating charge over all other assets.

This form of security must be registered with Companies House and such registration serves notice on subsequent potential lenders of the priority of the charge holder.

The main advantage of the fixed and floating charge is that it establishes the lender's claim in the assets of the company. The advantage of this form of security to the company is that it can continue to trade in (and with) the assets covered without the permission of the lender.

This advantage for the company is also the main drawback to the lender. Given that the company is free to deal with the assets, what assets will remain when the lender crystallizes the charge? This gives rise to a very important question, "How much is the charge worth?"

Another major disadvantage is that the company can create a fixed charge over assets currently covered by the floating charge. This fixed charge would take precedence over the floating charge even if it were created later. This can be overcome by creating a negative pledge as discussed in Chapter 6.

Let us look again at Alfa Ltd.

Table 8.1: Balance sheet of Alfa Ltd. as at 5 April 1999

				Captured by FFC
Fixed assets				
Freehold premises		45,000		Usually directly charged
Plant and machinery Cost	20,000			YES
Depreciation	5,000	15,000		
Motor vehicles Cost	12,000			YES
Depreciation	2,000	10,000	70,000	
Current assets				
Stock		21,000		YES – subject to Romalpa
Debtors		20,000		YES
Bank		2,500	43,500	
Current liabilities				
Creditors		23,500	23,500	
NET CURRENT ASSETS			**20,000**	
Long-term liabilities				
Loan		(15,000)	(15,000)	
TOTAL NET ASSETS			**75,000**	
Financed by				
50,000 £1 ordinary shares			50,000	
Retained profit			15,000	
Profit for the year			10,000	
			75,000	

Now, by extraction, we can summarize the assets covered under the charge:

Table 8.2: Partial balance sheet of Alfa Ltd. as at 5 April 1999

			Book value
Plant and machinery	Cost	20000	
	Depreciation	5000	15000
Motor vehicles	Cost	12000	
	Depreciation	2000	10000
Stock			21000
Debtors			20000
Value			66000

Is £66,000 a fair (and prudent) valuation?

No – for three main reasons.

1. As mentioned in earlier chapters, the accounts are out of date by the time we get them.

2. Even if up-to-date management accounts are used, there is still the problem of how accurate are the directors' values.

3. Even if the directors' values are accurate, will these values hold good if the business is in liquidation? Will all the debtors pay up in full? Will all the stock bring full value? Is some of the stock work-in-progress and thus requiring expenditure to make it saleable? Will the entire stock still be there? Can the plant, fixtures and fittings and vehicles be sold for their book values? How much can second-hand plant/cars be sold for?

All these questions mean that all fixed and floating charges are valued on a reduced value basis. For example:

Table 8.3

		Book Value		Reduction Factor[1]	
				%	
Plant and machinery	Cost	20000			
	Depreciation	5000	15000	60	9000
Motor vehicles	Cost	12000			
	Depreciation	2000	10000	50	5000
Stock			21000	40	8400
Debtors			20000	50	10000
Value			66000>>>>>>>>>32400		

Even this £34,000 is at best a guesstimate and will be further reduced if:

1. There are any preferential creditors. Their claim will take precedence.

2. The stock is subject to a Romalpa Clause. These clauses are based on *Aluminium Industrie Vaassen BV v. Romalpa Aluminium Ltd.* (1976). The effect of this case is that a supplier can amend its invoice such that "title to the goods does not pass to the buyer until he has paid for them." In brief, the supplier has gained *retention of title*. Such clauses are now very common and obviously reduce the value of stock.

If a lender does decide to take a fixed and floating charge (and most do), the lender first search Companies House to ensure that none of the assets covered by the charge have already been charged. If everything is in order, the lender registers the charge. As discussed the company remains free to deal in the assets and any new assets created become caught under the charge. This continues until the lender crystallizes the charge. Land not directly charged is also captured by the floating charge as are all other unmortgaged assets. Thus any assets purchased after the creation of the floating charge are captured if not directly charged.

8.2 Life policies

A life policy is a form of insurance under which an insurance company pays a guaranteed sum of money to the beneficiary of the policy on the death of the life insured. The beneficiary may be (and often is) the life assured. Altogether there are four parties to every life policy, with a possible fifth.

[1] These will vary from institution to institution.

1. *Proposer* – the person asking for the insurance cover.

2. *Assured* – the person whose death will lead to payment.

3. *Beneficiary* – the person who will get the funds.

4. *The insurance company* – the group that accepts the risk in return for a premium.

5. There may occasionally be a *trustee* for the policy.

The *policy document* details all the parties and is the essential document proving ownership in the benefits. Effectively the "title deeds".

The proposer, assured and beneficiary can be the same person. A man can effect a policy on his own life and in his favour, and his wife can also propose a policy on the husband and in her favour. Every proposer *must* have *insurable interest* in the assured. The test of insurable interest is "will the proposer suffer loss if the assured dies?" If the answer is yes, insurable interest exists. If the answer is no, then there is none. Another example is debtor/creditor. The creditor – being owed money – has an insurable interest in the debtor and can, therefore, effect a life policy so that the debt will be repaid in the event of the death of the debtor. The insurable interest is limited to the level of loss.

There are three main types of policies with which we will be concerned. These are term policies, endowment policies and whole of life policies

Term policies

All term policies have one main characteristic. They have a fixed expiry date and if death occurs before that time the sum assured is paid (tax free[2]) to the beneficiary or the estate of the assured. If the assured survives beyond the expiry date (by even one day!) the insurance company does not pay. If a lender has taken a charge over the policy the payment is forwarded to the lender. There are several forms of term assurance which lenders should be aware of.

The first is *decreasing-term assurance* (commonly called *mortgage protection policies*). These policies have an initial sum assured that is linked to a specific debt – usually a capital and interest mortgage. As repayments are made on the debt, the level of cover under the policy decreases at the same rate. Thus if a twenty-five-year £50,000 loan is made on 25 August 1999 and the assured dies on 26 August 1999, the insurance company pays the beneficiary £50,000. If, however, the assured dies on 24 August 2024, the insurance company will pay only the outstanding balance on the loan. This will be a few pounds at most.

If the debt is to be repaid in one lump sum, the decreasing-term policy is obviously the wrong choice. Here a lender would be looking for a *level-term policy*. Here, surprise, surprise, the cover remains the same throughout the term. Because the insurance company is liable for £50,000 on 26 August 1999 and £50,000 on 24 August 2024, the level-term policy has a higher premium than the twenty-five-year decreasing-term assurance.

There is also an *increasing-term policy*. Here the level of cover increases each year by some

---

[2] Subject to Inland Revenue qualifying rules.

predetermined measure (the retail price index or a fixed percentage are common). These are often used when the financial loss might increase over time. Suppose a company has a star executive who has produced increasing profits for the employer every year for the last five years. The death of this *key individual* could have serious financial consequences for the company while a replacement is found or trained. The main problem with *key man* policies is proving insurable interest and the level of such an interest. Having said that, the key man policy is a favoured form of security in many lending situations, especially when lending to partnerships and small companies.

We have already mentioned the main problem with term policies. If the assured dies after expiry date the beneficiary receives nothing. In many cases this is not a problem or concern, but the desire to provide a return on investment in the event of living beyond the expiry date led, many years ago, to the creation of the low-cost *endowment policy*.

An endowment policy, like a term policy, has a finite term during which, if death occurs, the guaranteed sum assured is paid to the beneficiary. After the expiry date a tax-free sum is also paid out. This sum is normally the sum assured. Thus if the following policy were effected – £50,000 endowment policy expiry date 25 August 2024 –

- dies before 25 August 2024, then £50,000 is paid out;

- lives until 25 August 2024, then £50,000 is paid out.

This £50,000 can be used for whatever purpose the beneficiary chooses. In fact, most polices of this nature are used in conjunction with interest-only mortgages with interest paid to a lender during the term and the lump sum used to repay the debt at maturity.

There are two types of endowment which differ primarily in their method of achieving the desired bullet repayment.

The traditional *with-profits endowment* accumulates value within the policy by a series of bonus payments which relate to the performance of the insurance company life fund. These bonuses[3] are made annually (reversionary bonuses) and at maturity (terminal). Annual bonuses are simple or compound[4]. The table below shows the difference in bonus accumulation from the two methods. Of the two methods, the greater surrender value is achieved by the compounded bonus method. Note that neither policy reaches £50,000 by the maturity date. The terminal bonus is designed to make up the shortfall. Some companies have a policy of extensive reliance on the terminal bonus – thus paying small reversionary bonuses – while other companies seek to build up larger bonuses through the lifetime of the endowment. A further note – the annual bonus rate need not, and rarely does, stay the same.

[3] Based on a percentage of the basic sum assured – this is lower than the guaranteed sum assured.
[4] Some companies operate a hybrid system.

Table 8.4

				Simple		Compound	
Basic sum Year	Bonus rate Assured	Bonus %	Bonus rate Total	Basis	%	Total
1	10000	4	10400	10000	4	10400
2	10000	4	10800	10400	4	10816
3	10000	4	11200	10816	4	11248.64
4	10000	4	11600	11248.64	4	11698.59
5	10000	4	12000	11698.59	4	12166.53
6	10000	4	12400	12166.53	4	12653.19
7	10000	4	12800	12653.19	4	13159.32
8	10000	4	13200	13159.32	4	13685.69
9	10000	4	13600	13685.69	4	14233.12
10	10000	4	14000	14233.12	4	14802.44
11	10000	4	14400	14802.44	4	15394.54
12	10000	4	14800	15394.54	4	16010.32
13	10000	4	15200	16010.32	4	16650.74
14	10000	4	15600	16650.74	4	17316.76
15	10000	4	16000	17316.76	4	18009.44
16	10000	4	16400	18009.44	4	18729.81
17	10000	4	16800	18729.81	4	19479
18	10000	4	17200	19479	4	20258.17
19	10000	4	17600	20258.17	4	21068.49
20	10000	4	18000	21068.49	4	21911.23
21	10000	4	18400	21911.23	4	22787.68
22	10000	4	18800	22787.68	4	23699.19
23	10000	4	19200	23699.19	4	24647.16
24	10000	4	19600	24647.16	4	25633.04
25	10000	4	20000	25633.04	4	26658.36

The policyholder has thus participated in the profits of the insurer. Once an annual bonus has been added it cannot be removed and forms the *surrender value* of the policy. These policies are widely held to be less risky than the *unit-linked* endowments because the insurer seeks to declare bonuses in such a manner as to even out the inevitable periods of good and bad profits which will be experienced over a normal twenty-five-year term. However, although the bonus programme will be geared to producing a tax-free sum in excess of the guaranteed sum assured at maturity, there are very few insurers who will guarantee this. The downside of this for a borrower is that after twenty-five years the endowment does not repay the mortgage debt. Many insurance companies and financial writers are currently concerned that the economic environment has changed so that investment returns (and thus profits and bonuses) will be less than in the 1980s and maturity values lower. Some companies are even suggesting that policyholders increase their premiums to overcome this possible shortfall.

Unit-linked endowments, while providing the same guaranteed sum assured, are structured differently. The maturity payout is produced by investing the policyholder's premiums in the stock market. Effectively the monthly premium (less cost of decreasing term assurance) is used to purchase units in one of the insurance company's unit trusts[5]. Each month the policyholder purchases new units and, over time, the units increase in price. This increase in price (and thus value) provides the maturity proceeds. The table below shows the basic effect. As unit prices increase the number of units bought decreases. But, and this is the key, all units are valued at the current rather than the purchase price.

Table 8.5

Monthly Investment	Cost Unit	Number Units	Total Units	Total Value
50	1	50	50	50
50	1.001	49.95	99.95005	100.05
50	1.002	49.9001	149.8502	150.15005
50	1.003	49.8503	199.7005	200.3002
50	1.004	49.8005	249.501	250.5005
50	1.005	49.7507	299.25175	300.751
50	1.006	49.701	348.95279	351.05175
50	1.007	49.6514	398.60419	401.4028
50	1.008	49.6018	448.20598	451.80421
50	1.009	49.5522	497.75823	502.25601
50	1.01	49.5027	547.26096	552.75827
550				562.76

[5] A type of investment that invests in other assets -predominately equities.

The danger is, however, that a unit price increase can easily become a unit price fall. Here you would buy more units but all would be valued at the lower price. In actual fact a period of low unit prices is good because it leads to a phenomenon known as *pound cost averaging*, which actually increases investment performance. Instead they have a fluctuating market value. However this feature of unit-linked policies means that they never achieve a guaranteed surrender value. In fact they have a fluctuating market value. The advantage claimed for unit-linked as opposed to with-profits endowments is that, theoretically, the value of units could exceed the debt before the loan expiry date. This obviously assumes consistent strong stock market performance over a long period. If this did occur a borrower could encash the policy and repay the debt. The interest payments and endowment premiums would cease, thus improving the disposable income of the customer.

Both types of endowment policy are widely used as security in home loan situations. The beneficiaries hand the policy document to the lender and create a legal charge over the policy. This is notified to the insurance company which notes the interest[6] of the lender and undertakes to remit proceeds to the lender either on death or maturity unless the charge has been released.

There will be situations where a customer has an endowment policy that is not linked in any way to a property purchase. It is a stand-alone portion of his or her investment portfolio. Because the surrender value in a with-profits policy is certain, the policy can be taken as security. For example, Mr and Mrs James wish to borrow £7,500 to go on a round-the-world cruise for their twenty-fifth wedding anniversary. They have a £12,500 with-profits endowment which has a premium of £25 p.m. This policy has a surrender vale of £8,000 and matures in two years with a projected maturity value of £15,000. They could surrender the policy and take the £8,000 but will lose out on the possible extra £7,000. Because the remaining premiums are only £600 they want to borrow the £7,500. Even if we assume a 15% interest rate on the debt for two years the customers will still be better off borrowing.

Projected return	Projected Premiums	Projected Interest	Surplus
7000	less (600 +	2250)	= 4150

We have two options:

If the customers can afford the interest costs of £93.75 p.m. then lending is no problem. If the customer cannot afford the interest payments we could roll up the interest and take the interest in a lump as well. Possible outcomes include:

- customers lives – policy pays up and we get repaid;

- customer dies – policy pays up and we get repaid;

- customer never comes back and cancels payment of premium. Because our interest in the policy has been noted by the insurance company we will be informed that payment of premiums has ceased. We can pay them until maturity and deduct the cost from the proceeds.

---

[6] This turns an equitable charge into a legal charge and establishes precedence.

- in the event of default the bank could sell the policy on the secondhand endowment to a specialized company.

If the policy were unit-linked as opposed to with-profits, the situation would be a little more complicated. Because the unit-linked policy has no guaranteed surrender value the lender has no guarantee of value. However the nature and structure of unit-linked investment means that lenders can have a degree of confidence in the likely minimum value of the policy. Different lenders take different viewpoints. However a lender that discounted the current value by twenty per cent would be reasonably prudent.

As stated, the use of endowment policies as security is well established. The problem with lending against any type of life policy with a surrender value[7] is that lenders can be so comforted by the surrender value that the normal canons of lending are ignored. Remember lending is totally different to pawnbroking.

Both term and endowment policies have a fixed term beyond which there is no life cover. Many years ago the life assurance industry developed whole-of-life policies, which cover the assured until death, whenever it occurs. These policies can be with-profits or unit-linked and can have surrender values (although the same restrictions apply).

When taking a life policy as security a number of points need to be borne in mind.

1. Is insurer a UK-based company?

2. Has the policy been set up properly? A prudent lender will check that the correct age has been detailed on the policy document and that the policy has been endorsed *age admitted*. The age is the primary factor an insurance company uses to set the sum assured and the premium. Had a customer taken out a policy and used the wrong date of birth the policy would be voided under the principal of *uberrimae fidei*[8].

3. Is the policy in trust? If it is the beneficiary will not receive the proceeds on death or maturity. These will be paid directly to the trustee. The solution is to ensure that the beneficiary and trustee sign the charge form. The most common form of trust is created when a policy has been effected under the Married Women's Property Act 1882. The most normal scenario is where a man takes out a policy on his own life[9] in favour of his wife and/or his wife and children. This wording creates the trust and may cause problems for taking the policy as an effective security. The problems are:

    - *Wife*: what happens in divorce situations. At the time of creation of the trust the wife may have been Mandy but on death the wife might be Alison. Does a charge form sign by Mandy bind Alison? *No*. The wife needs to be named.

    - *Children*: Are the children named? Are they over 18? If not can minors enter into a charge? *No*. For a valid charge the children need to be named and over eighteen.

  - The signing of the charge form by the beneficiaries must be witnessed and that witness should ideally be able to provide the beneficiaries with independent legal advice. This is

---

[7] N.B. Term policies do not have surrender values.
[8] A Latin term meaning utmost good faith. Essentially a proposer must not only answer all questions asked but also provide any information the insurer would find relevant even if not requested.
[9] He is proposer and assured.

to avoid the possibility of undue emotional pressure or influence being put on one or more of the beneficiaries. There are three famous (infamous?) cases where the question of undue influence has been examined.

- *Lloyds Bank Ltd. v. Bundy* (1975) – Undue influence of son on father. The father gave a guarantee for the son's bank account. The court eventually set the guarantee aside.[10]

- *Barclays Bank plc v. O'Brien* (1993) – Misrepresentation of the facts by Mr O'Brien to Mrs O'Brien. Mrs O'Brien entered into a legal charge jointly with her husband over the matrimonial home. This charge secured the overdraft of her husband's limited company. Although it could not be proven that Mr O'Brien had put his wife under emotional pressure, the House of Lords believed Mrs O'Brien's contention that she had been told that the sum involved was £60,000 (it was £130,000) and that it was for a period of three weeks (it was not). Mrs O'Brien was able to set aside the charge, because Barclays Bank had not insisted that she take independent legal advice.

- *CIBC Mortgage plc v. Pitt* (1993).

    Research time – what happened?

Table 8.6: Summary of life policies as security

Type	Term	Endowment
Fixed term	Yes	Yes
Surrender value	Never	With-profits – Guaranteed – Unit-linked – Variable
Suitable as security	Yes	Yes

Advantages	Disadvantages
Easy to complete formalities	*Uberrimae fidei* considerations
Easy to value	May need to make premiums if debtor does not.
Easy to realize	

8.3   Stocks and shares

These are financial assets issued by companies which can also be used as security for facilities. To recap from Chapter 2, a company can issued the following:

- ordinary shares;

[10] See later section on guarantees for full details.

- preference shares;

- loan stocks.

All of these can be acceptable forms of securities. The main advantages of these assets are that, like life policies, the procedure is reasonably simple (especially compared to land). They can be easy to value. Plc shares are often quoted on the stock exchange and it is thus possible to sell them without restriction and the share prices can be ascertained daily. However, as we are all aware, prices on stock exchanges can vary greatly and while it is simple to get today's value there is no guarantee that the value will be the same in seven days. A large price increase is obviously not a problem for a lender who is relying on the shares. A large fall is. A prudent lender will discount the value and each lender has its own discount rates. Unless the company is a blue-chip company, fifty per cent is considered prudent.

Unfortunately shares of unquoted (limited) companies are less easy to value, far more volatile in price, and may be covered by restrictions in transferability[11]. This obviously means that assessing a security value can be very, very difficult.

Loan stocks are also tradable on capital markets and prices can be obtained easily. Just as some shares are seen as being of better quality than others (British Telecom plc is better than Parry Mobiles plc), some loan stocks are considered better than others. The best form of loan stock to take as security is not debt issued by a company but rather that which has been issued by the UK government. These are universally known as gilt-edged stock (gilts for short). Gilts are extremely marketable, and while their market value can fluctuate, they have guaranteed income payments and guaranteed capital repayment at a fixed point in the future. For example, if we were offered £15,000 nominal of 7% Treasury Stock 2003 as security we would know the following with absolute certainty:

- income of £1,050 (£15,000 × 7%) paid in two instalments – ignoring tax;

- a capital repayment of £15,000 in 2003 (in practice we know the precise date).

Although we can calculate the interest due with the same precision for company loan stock, we can never have the same absolute certainty of receipt. Similarly there will always be some element of doubt with regards to the capital repayment with company debt, because both interest and capital repayment depend on the continued existence of the company.

The value of loan stock is calculated by multiplying the nominal value by the market price. Therefore as the market price changes, the value of the security changes. Again prudent lenders will discount the market value. The level of discount depends on the quality of the debt. Obviously gilts will have the lowest discount rate while the much maligned Parry plc will be discounted the most.

As with every form of security, a key aspect is the ability to prove that Mr X is in fact the owner and thus has the power to create the charge. With this type of financial assets there are several ways in which ownership can be proved.

The most common is the *share (or loan stock) certificate*. This details the name of the owner,

[11] In the company's articles of sssociation.

the type of share and the nominal value of the share[12]. The share certificate is issued by the company registrar. This is usually a bank or insurance company that keeps the details of shareholders for the company. The registrar amends the records of ownership only in receipt of a stock transfer form signed by the owner transferring his or her rights to a third party. Recent developments in the stock exchange have introduced a non-paper based system of ownership registration via *CREST*. Within CREST ownership is recorded electronically – the term *dematerialized*[13] is used to differentiate this form of recording from the paper-based system. Again ownership is transferred on the receipt of a CREST transfer form.

The majority of shareowners choose to have the shares registered in their own name but there are a few alternatives. Perhaps the most common alternative is to have the shares registered in a nominee name[14]. Effectively the nominee is the registered holder of the shares and receives all the dividends due. The nominee remits all the due dividends to the real owner. The main stated advantage for a nominee company is that an individual with a number of shareholdings need not be concerned with paperwork and tax calculations. Each nominee company obviously keeps records as to who owns what. If shares are registered in the name of a nominee, the owner loses the ancillary benefits that often accompany share ownership. Ownership in bearer form is also available, but this is becoming less popular. Open your wallet or purse and take out a note. If that note were stolen how would you be able to prove ownership? Shares and loan stocks issued in bearer form have the same drawbacks but are easy to transfer and mortgage.

Taking a mortgage over stocks and shares is simplicity itself. Stage one is to take possession of the share certificate. A memorandum of deposit and a signed undated stock transfer form are also taken. After these two stages an equitable mortgage has been created. This can be converted to a legal mortgage by depositing all the documents with the company registrar, who will issue a new certificate in the name of the lender.

Realizing the security is again very easy. Because the transfer form is signed and undated the shares can be sold at any time or simply passed into the ownership of the nominee company.

8.4   Guarantees and indemnities

A guarantee is a promise made (to a lender) to the effect that if the borrower does not repay then the guarantor will. Guarantees can be given by individuals, two or more people[15] – when liability is joint and several – and by companies (if the articles of association permit). Modern forms of bank guarantee incorporate an indemnity clause. This effectively binds the guarantor so that he or she is not able to avoid the debt on a technicality. Generally speaking guarantees are among the simplest forms of security to take because they are effected by

---

[12] Vital with preference shares because the dividend percentage is a percentage of the nominal value.

[13] Think Star Trek.

[14] Most financial institutions will have a nominee company called X Nominees Limited, where X is the name of the financial institution.

[15] Including partnerships provided all partners enter the guarantee.

simply signing the guarantee form. However, when taking guarantees the lender must be certain of a number of points:

- Does the guarantor have the legal capacity to enter into the guarantee? For example, minors and those deemed mentally incompetent are not able to give guarantees.

- Whose laws apply? Most guarantee forms contain a statement that the law of England governs the contract. In most cases this will suffice, However there can be difficulties if the guarantor is a foreign national. These primarily revolve around the capacity to contract which may be defined differently in other countries. For instance, the age of maturity in the UK is eighteen whereas in some other countries it is twenty-one or twenty-five.

- Has undue influence been placed on the guarantor?

  - *Lloyds Bank Ltd. v. Bundy* (1975) – Undue influence of a son on his father. The father gave a guarantee for the son's bank account. Bundy Senior gave a guarantee for £1,500 in favour of Lloyds Bank to secure the business account of Bundy Junior. The guarantee was supported by a mortgage over a domestic property. At a subsequent meeting of Bundy Senior, Junior and a bank official the guarantee was increased to £11,000. The son was made bankrupt by the bank who called on the guarantee. The High Court set the guarantee (and the mortgage) aside as Mr Bundy Senior was deemed to have been influenced to enter into a contract that benefited others.

  Subsequent to this landmark ruling (and the ruling in *Barclays v. O'Brien* which you will remember involved misrepresentation), lenders have invariably insisted that any guarantor has independent legal advice prior to entering into the guarantee. This prevents guarantors from avoiding a guarantee on the grounds that they did not understand what they were doing or did not appreciate the level of liability they were agreeing to guarantee. The legal adviser would normally make enquiries on the lender as to the current situation of the debtor which, providing the debtor agreed[16], would be disclosed. This enables the legal adviser to advise the potential guarantor that "the debtor is currently £45,000 overdrawn" or "the debtor is currently in credit". If the guarantee was for £50,000 this might have an influence on the guarantor.

- Is the guarantee actually worth anything? Guarantees are normally *all monies*, in which case the guarantor is covering all borrowing of the debtor, or *limited* to a specific maximum, but is the guarantor sufficiently financially strong to meet the liability? It is all very well my guaranteeing my son's overdraft of £100,000 but the words blood and stones spring to mind. How then can a lender determine the value, if any, of a guarantee? If the guarantor is a customer of the lender the problem is somewhat less because the lender will probably know something of the financial standing of the guarantor. If the guarantor is a customer of another financial institution a status enquiry would be the easiest method of trying to quantify financial standing. In many cases the lender seeks to have the guarantee supported by a legal mortgage over other assets that are easy to value. Normally this is by way of a second charge over property owned by the guarantor.

[16] If the debtor does not give permission no details can be released.

The value of the guarantee would in fact be the value of the tangibility of the security.

	No prior mortgage	**Prior Mortgage**
Value of property	100,000	100,000
Discount 75%	75,000	75,000
First mortgage	nil	50,000
Value of guarantee	75,000	25,000

If the second mortgage is taken to support the guarantee then the usual considerations and formalities will need to be followed (refer back to Chapters 6 and 7).

Once the guarantee is in place the lender can operate the account up to the extent of the guarantee. While the guarantee is in force the lender needs to remember that a duty of confidentiality is still owed to the debtor and the guarantor does not have rights, for example, to see statements or know how the account is being conducted. Of course, the guarantor can ask the lender to what extent the guarantee is being relied upon and there will one of three possible replies:

1. The guarantee is being fully relied upon – debt equals guarantee.

2. The guarantee is being relied upon to the extent of £X plus interest and charges but the position can change from day to day – debt less than guarantee.

3. The guarantee is not currently being relied upon but the situation can change day by day – debtor's account in credit.

The guarantor may decide on receipt of replies 2 or 3 to inform the lender that he or she is withdrawing the guarantee. However, such notice takes three months to become effective. Most guarantee forms contain a clause stating that the guarantee remains effective for three months after the death or mental incapacity of the guarantor. In such circumstances a claim can be made under the guarantee if the borrower cannot find alternative security.

The lender obviously has the right to call upon the guarantor for the full amount as and when required, or upon a lesser amount if he or she decides to terminate support to the debtor.

To summarize, guarantees are easy to take but difficult to value and often require additional security to make the guarantee worth anything.

8.5   Goods and produce

The use of goods and produce as security is widely seen in international trade and is a somewhat specialized area. International trade finance, its pitfalls, opportunities and specialized rules and documentation, is a study area in its own right and we shall not consider it in any depth here but we should look at the basic framework.

Lenders frequently provide finance to exporters (those selling goods abroad) and importers (those buying goods from abroad). As a scenario a lender may grant a produce loan for imported goods such as wool, cotton, wheat, etc. The importer issues specialized documents[17] and is financed by the lender until the goods are sold. The bank takes constructive possession of the goods being used as security by having them warehoused in its name or by taking possession of the title documents. There is very little in the way of formal security procedures and the quality of the security largely rest upon the customer, the shipper and the level of insurance attached to the goods.

Given the nature of most goods and produce, these types of loan are essentially short-term and repayment comes from the sale of the goods. Thus the lender is earning money quickly and repeatedly. It is not unusual to see a company with a revolving credit facility for its import/export activities in addition to their other facilities. Their short-term nature means that, while such things as inflation and interest rates are not going to directly effect the sale price, there might be other factors (especially with perishable goods) that could cause price fluctuations. Thus wide security margins in this field are common.

The main disadvantages in this type of security are:

- Initial valuation can be difficult. The importer will be buying and probably on-selling at a mark-up. The importer will often seek finance against the higher price.

- Insurance of the goods is essential and can be expensive, and a well-known insurer is a must.

- Warehousing of goods is usually necessary and this is an extra expense. The warehouser has a lien on the goods for unpaid costs.

- There may be a retention of title clause effected under the sale agreement.

The financing of import/export is essentially based on the underlying relationship between the customer and lender. And CAMPAR as opposed to CAMPARI is the key to the lending decision.

8.6   Conclusion

Over the course of this book we have looked together at the subject of lending and security. The constrictions of writing a textbook mean that the various considerations need to be sectionalized. However, the lending process is a tapestry. From the back all the knots and ties are clearly seen but from the front the work appears seamless.

As your experience and confidence increase you will notice that you are making the tapestry from the front rather than the rear. This integration of your skills and knowledge can only come from practice and I would encourage you to work through all the examples, both in this text and the accompanying workbook, until you understand them. Another excellent source of understanding is senior colleagues. Trust me when I say that they will love to recount their successful *deals*. Listen patiently to them and eventually they will start to recount tales of

[17] Documentary credits, documents for collection, etc.

lesser success. Other people's mistakes are a wonderful source of knowledge. However, as I said in Chapter 1, you will one day make a mistake of your own and lose money. Then you will really to start to learn.

It is highly likely that you will be sitting an exam in this area. This will be testing your understanding and the application of your knowledge and I strongly suspect that you will get very few marks for repeating huge chunks of the text.

I close by wishing you success in your future lending career.

Appendix 1

THE TRICK IS KNOWING WHEN NOT TO LEND

For my sermon today, I take as my text the story of the seven fat years, when the harvests were good, followed by the seven lean years, when times were hard. As far as we are concerned the fat years began, of course, in 1982, when the government abolished remaining hire purchase controls. Suddenly, neither credit nor longer-term borrowing was rationed by government edict. Suddenly, it seemed, we could all have a wallet bulging with plastic cards, with a personal loan or two on top, and, naturally, a big fat mortgage.

For lenders it was a period of marvellous invention and innovation. For borrowers it was the financial equivalent of kids being let loose in a sweet shop and told to get on with it. Not surprisingly, at the end of the process both sides felt more than a little sick.

The lean years started in 1989, when sharply rising interest rates doubled the cost, for borrowers, of servicing their loans and it became apparent, for the first time in living memory, that house prices could go down as well as up. People had climbed the old debt mountain and when they looked down from the top, they got vertigo. Borrowers shunned new debt and lenders, nursing too high a proportion of non-performing loans (that is, ones that disappeared down the plughole), drew in their horns. Lessons had been learned. The same thing would never happen again.

The seven years are, however, over. The housing market is showing a decisive recovery in activity and a rather bigger recovery in prices. Normal service, which for most people means house prices outstripping general inflation, has been resumed. And it has been resumed, too, for the lenders. Remember negative equity? Forget it. Remember all those head-office memos urging a highly cautious approach to new loans? They are filed under 'N' for 'no longer relevant'.

There are mortgage offers out there which, for the life of me, I cannot see will make any money – and this is without allowing for a proportion of bad debts. It is a better time for borrowers than anything I remember in the late 1980s. True, the aim may be to get people in through the front door and make sure they stay in. And true, the level of scrutiny, of both the borrower's circumstances and the value of the property on which the loan is being made, are more rigorous than it was in the boom years. At least I hope it is.

I do, however, sympathise with lenders. The present situation, with house prices set for at least a couple of years of 10 per cent-plus rises, is a genuinely difficult one. The last thing they want to do is miss out on new and potentially lucrative business, which means competing by cutting margins. But they don't want to get sucked into the 1980s trap again of lending too much to the wrong people just because others are doing so.

As it is for the mortgage market, so for the other forms of lending. My biggest mailbag at home is in the form of offers to take out personal loans (usually marketed as featuring some new flexibility), or to take on another credit card, always with 'very low interest rates and no annual fee'. I would like to think this is because I am an excellent credit risk – but I doubt it. Mail-shots are not usually so selective.

Something is happening. Official figures show that bank and building society lending was running at more than £7bn a month in late 1996, almost double its level a year earlier. Business is booming. Is it another seven fat years, or will it be two or three?

For some people, the strong growth in bank and building society lending, which has propelled money supply growth back into double figures, is a sign, not only of a big inflationary cloud on the horizon, but also that the constraints of the first half of the 1990s are giving way to recklessness on both sides of the lending equation. Memories, after all, can be short.

There is, in addition, more competition now than in the1980s. Any lender taking an excessively cautious view risks ending up looking like an old maid. Taking a middle line, that is picking up new business while keeping tight controls on quality, is a difficult balancing act. It will be easy to fall off.

All my instincts tell me that the experience of the late 1980s was a one-off, brought about by the combination of an unusual economic environment – including big tax cuts – and the first strong upturn to occur in an era of financial liberalization. Self-imposed restraint, partly as a result of that experience, will, during this recovery, replace the earlier formal controls.

The growth of lending, while looking strong at present, will occupy a middle path between the runaway boom of that period, and the previous, more modest, tightly-rationed expansion.

That does not mean, however, that the present situation is without risk. There are younger borrowers who were not around to have their fingers burned during boom time, and there are also newer lenders in the market. The trick for older hands is knowing when to lend during the good times but also, more importantly, knowing when not to.

David Smith
Chartered Banker **March 1997**

Index

A

ability 15, 26, 29, 35, 142
accident sickness redundancy 20, 36
accountant 13, 16
Accounting
    adjustments 104
    concepts 95
    Standards Board 101
accounts 29, 53, 70, 113, 124
accrual 96
accruals concept 95
acid
    ratios 141
    acid test ratio 132, 136, 140
administration costs 122
administrators 45, 46
aged list of
    creditors 103
    debtors 102, 129, 141
agreed settlement 93
all monies 150
Alternative
    current cost accounting basis 125
    Investment Market 52
Aluminium Industrie Vaassen BV v Romalpa Aluminium 169
amount 18, 26, 29, 35, 142
    of equity 81
annual
    general meeting 52, 55, 111, 133
    percentage rate (APR) 37
arrangement fees 22
articles of association 55, 178
asset 19, 39, 46, 58, 97
    holder 145
    purchase 17, 60, 119
    real 73
    stripping 129
    turnover period 128
    Utilisation Ratios 136
    valuation 125
    value 125
    virtual 73
assignment 157, 159
associations 13, 40, 45
assured 170
attachment of earnings order 93

AVCO *see* average cost
Aveling Barford Ltd v. Perion Ltd (1989) 154
average cost (AVCO) 100, 101

B

bad debts 17, 20, 92, 141
balance sheet 57, 97, 98, 99, 104, 105, 106, 111, 113, 123, 133
bank 12
    account 129
bankrupt 49
bankruptcy 48, 51, 57, 94, 131, 151
Barclays Bank plc v. O'Brien 162, 176, 179
base rate 17, 30
bearer form ownership 178
beneficiary 170, 171
Bernstein, Peter 15
board of directors 52, 55, 131
bonus 67, 171
borrower 12, 37, 39
borrowing 59
    capacity 45
both or all to sign mandates 45
bouncing 91
    cheques 15
brand 99
Brandao v. Barrett (1846) 146
bridging
    finance 13
    loan 82, 83
budget planner 18
Buffet, William 113
building society 12, 39
buildings 97
bullet repayment 80
business
    accounts 49
    borrowing 84
    expansion 87
    overdraft 68
        facility 70
    plan 16
    start-up or buy-out 17
    transfer agency 29
    valuation report 29

C

CAMPAR 181
CAMPARI 14, 21, 26, 29, 36, 37, 142, 155, 181
capacity to contract 43
capital 56, 92, 103
    account 104
    and interest mortgage 79, 170
    repayment holidays 88
    structure 126
capped rate 80
car purchase 72
CASCAR 149
cash 99
    flow 30, 113, 115
        forecast 69, 116, 118
        problem 60
        statement 113, 114
Catlin v. Cyprus Finance Corporation (London) Limited 42, 43
CCCPARTS 14, 21
certificate of incorporation 54
character 14, 15, 26, 29, 35, 37, 142
charge
    card 61
    certificate 160
    form 156, 162, 175
Charges Registry 160
charging order 93
charity 13, 45
cheque 62, 91
    card 91
    guarantee provisions 91
chief executive 52
CIBC Mortgage Plc v Pitt 176
City of London Building Society v. Flegg 161
Clayton's Case 150
clean 115
club 45
    mandate 46
clubs 13, 40, 46
collared rate 80
commission 22
Companies Act
    1985 53, 55, 101
    1989 53, 114
        S35B 55
Companies House 53, 144, 145, 166, 169
company 104, 151, 156
    cars 97
    funding 56
    registrar 178

compounded bonus method 171
compulsory liquidation 57
conduit 13
consistency 99, 101
    concept 95
constructive possession 181
Consumer Credit Act 1974 37, 78
continuing security 149
    clause 150
contract 43, 54
convertible
    loan stock 132
    preference shares 56, 132
conveyance 157, 159
corporate
    lending 16
    veil 51
cost of goods sold 134
cost/benefit analysis 85
covenants 148
credit
    card 16, 17, 44, 61, 71, 74
    given 140
    limit 61
    payment period 129
    reference
        agency 41
        search 41
    scoring 10, 36, 37
        systems 20
creditors 37, 48, 57, 114, 124
    with security 58
creditworthiness 66
CREST 178
    transfer form 178
cross firing 24, 92
cumulative prefs 56
current
    account 22, 61, 99, 102, 104, 116
    assets 99
    cost accounting 125
    liabilities 102
    /acid ratios 141
customer categories 39
CV 84

D

David Copperfield 60
debenture 57, 123
debit card 62, 72
debt consolidation 73
debtor

book 89
    collection period 136
debtors 37, 101, 114, 117, 123
decreasing term assurance 170
deed of priorities 163
deeds 161
Department of Trade and Industry 88
deposit 18
depreciation 98, 99, 114, 123, 125
    charge 99
derivatives 76
direct
    charge form 161
    debit 61, 91
    security 144, 145
director 52, 54, 55, 84, 131
discounted rate 80
distribution costs 122
District Land Registries (DLR) 144, 156, 160-
    164
dividend 56, 124
dividend
    cover 133
    per share 133
    yield 133
dividends 103, 111
DLR *see* District Land Registries
double entry concept 95
doubtful debt 92, 102

E

earnings per share 132, 133
educational qualifications 16
electronic point-of-sale (EPOS) technology 62
endowment policy 80, 171, 174, 175, 176
Equifax Europe Ltd 41
equitable
    charge 161
    mortgage 147, 148, 178
exceptions report 67
execution of assets 93
executor 13, 40, 45, 46
expediency 21
expenses 116
Experian Ltd 41
exporters 181

F

facility 13
    fees 22
factor 89

factoring 89
Family Law Reform Act 1969 43
fee 157
FIFO 100, 101
Financial
    advisors 13
    assets 73
    Reporting Standards (FRSs 96
    Times 52
first
    impressions 15
    in first out (FIFO) 100
fixed
    and floating charge 146, 151,168
    assets 97, 98, 102, 114, 125, 126, 128
        intangible 99
    charges 145
    cost 116
    interest debt 126
    rate 80
fixtures and fittings 97
floating charge 145
    holders 58
fluctuating balance account 61
forced sale valuation 156
forecast figures 115
forecasting 90
foreclosure 164
formal letter 93
franchising 89, 90
freehold 123, 157, 158, 159
    land 157
freeholder 158, 160
FRS 124
fully diluted earnings per share 132

G

garnishee order 93
gearing 127, 136, 139
general
    and special meetings 55
    lien 146
gilt 177
    -edged stock 177
gilts 57, 177
going concern concept 95
goods and produce 180
goodwill 29, 34, 99
grant of probate 46
gross
    margins 92
    profit 100, 101

margin 130, 136, 140
ground rent 160
guarantee 46, 47, 82, 88, 143, 146, 178, 179
guarantees and indemnities 178
guarantor 178, 179, 180

H

hard core 68, 87
    borrowing 68
    overdrawn position 67
    position 70, 90
head lease 158, 160
hire purchase 89, 103, 127
historic cost account basis 125
home improvements 73
house mortgages 16

I

identification 41
IHT threshold 79
illness 20, 74
importers 181
in case of need overdraft facility 70
indemnities 178
indemnity clause 178
independent legal advice 179
individual accounts 40
inflation 125
    accounting 125
inheritance tax 46
    threshold 78
Inland Revenue 45, 78, 79, 103
Insolvency Act 1986 131
    Section 214 131
Insolvency Rules 1986 131
insolvent 131
    Partnerships Order 1994 51
institutional investors 52
insurable interest 170
insurance 19, 20, 26, 30, 36, 37, 156, 181
    company 12, 82, 159, 162, 170
    policy 162, 163
intangible fixed assets 99
inter-firm comparison 125
interest 22, 111
    cover 126, 136, 141
    rate 20, 39
        swaps 76
    -only 80
        mortgages 171
international trade 87

intestate 46
introducer 13, 43
investment 132
    ratios 132
ISA 80

J

joint account 41, 43, 49
    mandate 41
    and several 178
        liability 42, 45, 51
    liability 44, 50
    tenancy 157, 161

K

key
    individual 171
    personnel 84

L

LA bonds 57
land 97, 146
    certificate 146, 155, 160, 161, 162
    Charges Department 161, 163, 164
    Registration Act 1925 160
last in first out (LIFO) 100
Law of
    Property Act 1925 147, 157
        Section 101 151
        Section 103 151
lawyer 16
leasee 158
leasehold 157, 158, 159
    Reform Act 1967 160
leaseholder 158
leasing 127
leasor 158
legal
    charge 174
    interest 144
    mortgage 145, 147, 161, 178, 179
lending 10
    equation 12
lessor 103
level term policy 170
liabilities 53, 102, 103
LIBOR *see* London Inter-Bank Offered Rate
lien 146, 181
life
    insurance 22
    policies 146, 169, 176

LIFO 100
limited company 13, 51, 54, 55, 89, 127, 151
limited partners 50
liquidation 57, 131, 151, 168
liquidator 57, 58, 131, 151, 154
    expenses 58
liquidity 17, 39, 60, 131, 136
    needs 60
    problem 60
Lloyds Bank 179
Lloyds Bank Ltd. v Bundy 162, 176, 179
Lloyds Bank Plc v. Rossett 161
loan 22
    accounts 72
    facilities 74
    stock 57, 177
    stock certificate 177
    loan to value (LTV 82
local authority search 162
London Inter-Bank Offered Rate (LIBOR) 16
long term
    capital 57
    loans 79
    liabilities 102

M

management accounts 90, 92, 124
mandates 45, 50
Mareva Injunction 93
margin 16, 20, 26, 29, 30, 35, 142
mark up 121
Married Women's Property Act 1882 175
MARS 14, 21
materiality concept 95
Matrimonial Homes Act (1983) 162
memorandum of
    association 54
    deposit 147, 178
MGI 82
Midland Bank Ltd v. Dobson 161
minor 44, 45
Minor Contracts Act 1987 44
Minors 43
MIP *see* mortgage guarantee indemnity
mnemonic 14, 15, 19, 164
Monetary Policy Committee 80
money measurement concept 96
monitoring facilities 90
mortgage 146, 158, 159, 164, 173, 178, 179
    form 161
    guarantee indemnity 165
    guarantee indemnity policy (MGI) 82

loans 13
    protection policies 170
mortgagee 146, 147, 149, 154, 156, 160, 161, 162
    in possession 164
mortgages 79
mortgagor 146, 147, 154, 156, 160, 163

N

negative
    equity 18, 156
    pledge 167
net
    asset value 29
    gearing 127, 136
    profit 134
        margin 130, 133, 134, 136, 140
    realisable value 101
    worth 103, 126
new business start-up 87
nominee
    company 178
    name 178
non-trading partnerships 49

O

objects clause 55
obsolescence 101
open market valuation 156
operating
    margin 130, 136
    profit 114
opportunities 85
ordinary shares 56, 104, 132
overdraft 13, 21, 22, 65, 73, 80, 87, 90, 91, 102, 116, 118, 129, 148
    facility 21, 30, 67, 87
    limit 91, 92
overtrading 92
owner's capital 18

P

PARSER 14, 21
participating preference shares 56
particular lien 146
partly-paid shares 53
partner 50, 131
partnership 12, 16, 49, 51, 53, 103, 104, 131, 151, 171
Partnership Act 50
pawnbroking 19, 31

pension plan 80
PEP 80
 mortgage 80
permanent health insurance 20
personal
 account 40, 41, 45
 loan 13, 16, 78
  application forms 19
 overdrafts 16
plant and machinery 97
 purchase 88
plc 133
pledge 145
policy document 170
possession 164
pound cost averaging 174
preference 154
 shares 56, 104
preferential creditor 58, 103, 169
primary financial statements 113, 114
private limited companies 51, 52, 56, 133
probate loan 78, 79
process 13
produce loan 181
profit and loss account 95, 99, 101, 107, 123, 129
profitability 129
profits 19, 56, 103, 111
projected
 balance sheet 115
 profit and loss account 115
property 97, 99, 151
proposed dividend 111
proposer 170
prudence 101
 concept 96
public limited companies 13, 52, 124
puisne mortgage 159
purpose 17, 26, 29, 35, 142

Q

quarterly fee 45

R

ratio analysis 124
Re. M.C. Bacon 131
receiver 46, 164
redeemable preference shares 56
reducing balance
 basis 74
 depreciation 98

redundancy 20
registered land 160, 161
Registered Office 54
registered title 158
Registrar of Companies 55
remuneration 22
rental income 97
repayment 18, 30, 35, 142
 mortgage 79
repaymentability 26
research and development 99
reserves 104
retail price index 171
retained profits 111, 133
retention of title 169, 181
return on capital employed 130
revaluation 99
 reserve 99, 104, 123
reversionary bonuses 171
revolving credit 13, 61, 73, 79, 89, 142, 147, 149, 181
right of way 158
rights issue 73
risk 17, 20, 142
ROCE 130
Romalpa Clause 169

S

SAL 68, 70, 74
salaried partners 50
salary 18, 20, 67
 anticipation limit (SAL) 65
 multiplier 81
sales 128
 budget 115
 /fixed assets 140
Saloman v. Saloman & Co Ltd 51, 53
secretary 52
Section 251 Insolvency Act 19986 131
security 15, 17, 19, 20, 21, 30, 31, 142, 143, 148, 151, 171, 176, 178, 181
 documentation procedures 154
 values 143
separate entity concept 96
set-off 42, 43
shadow director 131
share
 capital 52, 123
 certificate 146, 177, 178
shareholder 52, 53, 54, 55, 56, 58, 124, 127, 131, 132, 154, 178
shares 56, 104, 176, 178

shipper 181
Siebe Gorman & Co Ltd v Barclays Bank Ltd
    166
signature 41, 43
sleeping partners 50
small firms loan guarantee scheme (SFLGS) 88
Small Loans Arrangement Scheme (SLAS) 88
sole
    account 43, 48
    trader 12, 16, 41, 43, 44, 53, 103, 104,
        131
solicitors 13
SORG 113
SSAP 98, 101, 124
Standard Chartered Bank v Walker and Walker
    164
standing order 54, 62, 91

statement of
    recognised gains and losses 97, 113
    shareholder liability 55
    Standard Accounting Practice (SSAPs)
        96
status enquiry 179
stock 100, 116
    transfer form 178
    turnover 140, 141
    turnover period 128, 134, 136
    valuation 30, 134
    values 140
stocking
    facilities 88
    loans 87
stocks 178
    and shares 73, 146, 176, 178
straight line depreciation 98
strengths 85
sub-lease 158
subrogation 82
successor 151
surrender value 175
SWOT 86
    analysis 85

T

Table A 55
tangible assets 98
tax 103
tenants in common 157, 161
term
    assurance 170
    loan 87, 142

policy 170, 175, 176
terminal bonus 171
testator 45
third party 143, 144, 147, 154
    charge form 161
    security 144
threats 85
time share purchase 72
title
    deed 155, 156, 160
    documents 181
total assets 126
trade creditors 102
trademark 99
trading
    and profit and loss account 97, 106, 109,
        113, 137
    certificate 54
    partnerships 49
transactions under value 154
trust deed 45
trustee 45, 170, 175
    in bankruptcy 48, 54, 151
trustees 13, 40
turnover 29, 128
    charge 22
    fee 45

U

uberrimae fidei 175, 176
ultra vires 55
undischarged bankrupt 48, 49, 54
unemployment 74
unit trusts 173
unit-linked
    endowment 173, 174
    policy 175
unregistered
    land 160, 161, 163
    title 158
unsecured
    basis 142
    creditor 58, 154
    debt 58

V

valuation 155, 156, 161, 162
value
    financial 143
    value in use 143
    of security 81

valuer 81, 99, 156, 161, 162
variable
  cost 116
  rates 80
vehicles 97

W

warehousing 181

warrants 57, 132
weaknesses 85
whole-of-life policies 175
will 45, 46
Williams and Glyn Bank Ltd v Borland 161
with-profits endowment 171, 174
working capital 105, 119, 123
  ratio 132, 136
writs 54